Everyone Is Welcome

Everyone *Is* Welcome

Creating a Culture of Inclusion in Congregational Schools

STEVEN H. RAU
STACEY LEVY

URJ Press
New York

to

To Benjamin Faber, the most gifted teacher of inclusion,
who continually teaches us to be sure that everyone is welcome.

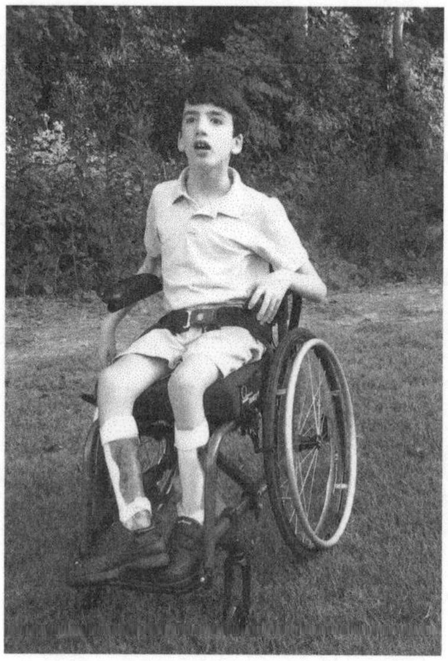

For permission to reprint, please contact:
URJ Press
633 Third Avenue
New York, NY 10017-6778
212-650-4120
press@urj.org

"Benjamin" from *Chicken Soup for the Teacher's Soul*, reprinted with permission.
"Welcome to Holland" by Emily Perl Kingsley, reprinted with permission.

Printed on acid-free paper

Manufactured in the United States of America

10 9 8 7 6 5 4 3 2 1

Everyone Is Welcome

Contents

Introduction

The great Chasidic master Rabbi Nachman of Breslov taught about a young prince who was convinced that he was a rooster. At first his parents—the king and queen—thought the prince was kidding. They began to worry, however, when, instead of joining them at the royal table, he would crouch down like a rooster, naked, underneath a table in the garden, and insist on clucking and eating only chicken feed.

At first they tried to ignore him, thinking that he would come out from beneath the table after a couple of days, but soon they realized that nothing they could do was going to cure him. As word traveled around town, the prince's behavior became the talk of the kingdom. The royal couple grew so embarrassed that they did not even want to leave the gates of the palace. The king called upon the services of the finest physicians and healers, sparing no expense to cure his son. But with each new method, his son slipped deeper into the belief that he was a rooster.

One day, a gentle rabbi arrived at the palace door, claiming that he had the ability to cure the prince. The king and queen, who were desperate by this point, told the rabbi that they were willing to pay him whatever he wanted. He responded that he would do it for free on the condition that no one interfered with any of his work.

Immediately, the rabbi undressed, climbed down below the table, and began pecking at chicken feed beside the prince. Curious, the prince clucked angrily, inquiring why the rabbi was there next to him. The rabbi calmly responded in his best clucking voice, "I am a rooster, and this is where roosters hang out in the kingdom." Slowly, the two got to know each other, and soon the prince began to enjoy the rabbi's company.

After a couple of days, the rabbi put on a pair of pants and continued to peck at the chicken feed. The prince, curious once again, asked the rabbi why a rooster would be wearing pants. The rabbi replied, "Who says that a rooster cannot wear pants? This stone floor is cold. Why should the humans be the only ones who wear pants?" The prince, shivering against the stone floor, picked up his pants and put them on as well.

The king and queen were astonished to see that the rabbi was making progress with their son. They were even more overjoyed as each day over the next week the rabbi made further advances, getting the prince to wear a shirt, socks, shoes, and a belt. Yet he still was bent down with the rabbi, pecking at chicken feed and clucking.

The following day, the rabbi clucked a story to the boy, telling him that in the land where he came from, roosters stand upright and eat their feed at a table. Trusting in his new friend, the prince came out from underneath the patio table and walked upright inside the house until he sat down at the royal table. As the chef began bringing out people food, the rabbi quickly signaled for him to bring the boy a plate of chicken feed. When the rabbi began eating people food, the prince once again objected, "You can't eat that. It is for people." The rabbi replied, "Oh. Didn't I tell you that in my country chickens eat people food?" Sure enough, the prince began eating regular food.

Within a couple of weeks, the rooster prince was wearing clothes, speaking, walking, and eating people food. While he still believed that he was a rooster, he conducted himself just like a human being.

Though this Chasidic story may sound a bit far-fetched, it holds a powerful message for educators and congregations. Almost two hundred years ago, Rabbi Nachman of Breslov taught that with patient and creative teachers—those who are able to bend down to the level of their students—children who are different could be taught to live in the world with their peers. By climbing under the table and learning about the rooster prince, the rabbi was gradually able to bring this child to the dinner table with his family. Over the last two decades, educators in North America have started to understand this idea. More and more, they are taking students who learn differently out of special classrooms and including them in the same classrooms as their peers.

The Hebrew word for synagogue, *beit k'nesset*, reminds us that the primary role of a congregation is to be a place of "gathering." However, many congregations unknowingly set up barriers for families by restricting access to their educational programs. In a time when congregations are struggling financially and are searching for ways to recruit new members, we are inadvertently discouraging some prospective members by not addressing families of children with special needs.[1] Once we can set aside our fears of educating these students, congregational educators can instead recruit and welcome them into our mainstream programs.

As society is becoming more aware of and knowledgeable about the wide array of learning styles and the importance of accommodating those with specific special needs, coupled with synagogues' need to retain and recruit members, it is even more crucial for congregations to welcome all types of learners and especially those with special needs into our programs. The Jewish community and the synagogue, in particular, should be leading the charge for educating all children equally. Like the rabbi in the story, we as educators must climb underneath the table to reach out to these children and their families, to welcome them and help them better fit in to our synagogue communities.

Almost fifteen years ago, a parent of a fourth-grade boy with dyslexia entered my of-

1 At the outset of this book, it is most important for us to mention our philosophy regarding the use of the term *special needs*. Though the philosophy is discussed in depth in chapter 2, we want to state early on that we rarely use isolating terms for students when speaking to parents, teachers, and staff. Labeling a child as "special" often makes parents uncomfortable. For the sake of clarity, we use the term "special needs" throughout the book as it is currently the most universally accepted term for the range of diagnoses it describes.

fice to inform me that she had decided to pull her son out of Hebrew school because he was not capable of learning Hebrew. As a new rabbi, I told her not to worry because we would get him the proper help. Truth be told, I had no idea what I was going to do. Like most Jewish educators, I had a solid background in educational theory and had touched briefly on special needs in my studies. However, I did not have any formal training working with youngsters with special needs, especially not when teaching Judaics and a second language. But as a Jewish educator, I innately knew that, regardless of how much Hebrew this child would learn, both he and his family needed our religious school to give this youngster a positive experience, so that he could develop a lifelong sense of Jewish pride. After making several calls to some of my senior colleagues, I learned that there were very few resources regarding educating children with special needs in religious or Hebrew school settings. Luckily, I came across a teacher in my program experienced in special needs education. Together, we created a self-contained Hebrew class for students with special needs in fourth, fifth, and sixth grades, with the goal of preparing them for bar and bat mitzvah. These students learned with their peers during religious school and studied separately during Hebrew school.

Though a short-term problem had been solved, I quickly discovered that there was a much larger problem in Jewish education—the lack of knowledge, training, and tools for educators to welcome children into their schools who have physical, emotional, behavioral, cognitive/social, or academic special needs. What would I have done if this teacher had left? How would I have reacted if I were approached by a parent of a child with Down syndrome, knowing that my program could not meet the more complicated physical and developmental needs of such a child?

When I moved to Atlanta in 2002, the challenge I feared emerged. Only one week after I arrived, a frustrated mother and father of a four-year-old, nonverbal child in a wheelchair, who had mitochondrial disease, met with me to share their history of being "denied." Over the first four years of their son's life, they were "denied" by almost every Jewish organization or educational institution they had approached. The leaders of these organizations had each begun the conversation by telling the parents what their child could *not* do. Regarding Jewish education, they were told that the only option for him was a small community Sunday school for students with severe needs. Praying for a small miracle, I told these parents that we would work to include their child in our program.

Unfortunately, this family's experience is all too common. At most educational institutions around the country, families who have children with special needs are rejected. We as Jewish educators must reverse his trend within our organizations. Families need to know that our congregations are safe places for all students, no matter their differences or special needs.

Within weeks of meeting this family, I began consulting with Stacey Levy, a local speech-language pathologist with strong professional experience in special education. She was tutoring several bar and bat mitzvah students with identified special needs in our congregation. Starting with one four-year-old child, we began creating a program that developed over the following years for students of all ages with a wide range of disabilities and special needs. This program includes:

- Professional development for teachers working with students with special needs
- Giving teachers and learning assistants working with each identified child a written document spelling out background information on the child and proposed classroom strategies
- A program for identifying and training *madrichim* (high school students who volunteer as teaching assistants) to

shadow students with special needs or provide one-on-one support for a number of students in the school with special needs
- An on-site learning lab that prepares students for success in the classroom, both on site and at satellite locations
- An on-site supervisor who serves a resource for teachers and parents

With each new child joining the program over the first few years, Stacey's eyes would light up. She would create a written plan for the classroom teacher and the *madrichim*. The plan suggested some simple classroom modifications to serve the child's needs. All of a sudden, rather than complaining, our teachers were proudly sharing success stories of these children in their classrooms.

The more difficult the needs, the more creative the modifications and suggestions Stacey would develop. Though most of the modifications were successful, some of them failed. But each new student who entered the program provided a new challenge for Stacey. Much like the rabbi who worked with the rooster prince, Stacey would first attempt a new strategy before proposing it to the teachers or the *madrichim*.

The success of one particularly challenging student with autistic behaviors reinforced the importance of this program. This child had been adopted from a Russian orphanage, where he had received almost no physical contact as an infant. Studies have shown that children raised without touch of any kind often develop significant psychological and learning-based special needs. Part of this child's diagnosis included sensory processing issues that made him especially sensitive to loud noises and large crowds. In anticipation of starting on Sunday mornings, Stacey asked his parents to bring him to visit his Sunday school classroom several times before the first day of class. To prevent the child from having a negative reaction to the hustle and bustle of the first day, Stacey met the child outside his classroom a half hour before class, along with a *madrich*. When he refused to enter the classroom, Stacey and the *madrich* attempted several strategies to get him inside—positive reinforcement, giving him small toys and trinkets, and promises of extra computer time at home. When she realized that none of these tempted him, Stacey pulled out a deck of cards and starting building a card maze, domino-style, leading into the classroom. The boy was fascinated by the standing cards and focused intensely on the interesting distraction. Slowly, he followed the cards into the classroom. When Stacey asked him to push the cards down, he laughed with delight as the cards fell. Once inside the classroom, he was captivated by all the engaging classroom decorations. As the *madrich* led him to explore other parts of the room, he forgot about his fear of entering. Soon, he and the *madrich* were seated at the table with other second graders. While each day presented a new set of challenges, had it not been for Stacey's persistence, this child would never have attended religious school. Five years later, he became bar mitzvah, reading from the Torah with a special tapping rhythm strategy developed by Stacey.[2]

Over the first few years of our work together, the scope of the program became larger than we could imagine. As parents shared their children's success stories around the community, we were soon receiving phone calls from parents and educators from other congregations around the United States and Canada who had learned of our program by word of mouth. Over and over again, we heard the sad news that most congregations simply do not accommodate children with special needs. When we inquired as to why

2 In addition to his Hebrew learning strategy, Stacey worked with the rabbi to create a *Star Wars* incentive system. This helped the child connect with the rabbi as they discussed *Star Wars* frequently during his bar mitvah studies, and he had a *Star Wars* action figure next to him when he read from the Torah.

not, the answers were typically the same: money and resources.

Because of what we have heard from other educators, we have been sharing methodology locally and nationally for years, explaining that creating an inclusive educational program does not necessarily require additional funding. This book, including the curriculum for training *madrichim* (whom we have termed *tzadikim*)[3], is designed to help Jewish educators work with their faculty and staff to climb underneath the table or pull out a deck of cards to welcome all students into congregational learning. No matter the size or budget of a congregation, it is time to put aside our fear of bringing children who learn differently into our programs and develop a whole new philosophy in our community. The truth is, we all learn differently. As we learn from Dr. Howard Gardner,[4] we each process information best through one or more of eight types of intelligences. Some of us are visual learners, while others are auditory. Most of us learn to compensate for our differences and adjust to the style being taught. But those who struggle because of their special needs should not have to overcompensate in a traditional classroom or be separated from the rest of their community. Learning from our tradition, together we can make the prophet Isaiah's words a reality, so that our houses "shall be called a house of prayer for all peoples" (Isaiah 56:7) and all of our "children shall be students of Adonai" (Isaiah 54:13).

Rabbi Steven H. Rau, RJE

3 The training curriculum introduces high school students to the term *tzadikim*, meaning "righteous individuals." Because of their altruistic volunteer work with children with special needs, we believe the *madrichim* earn this title.

4 In 1983, Dr. Howard Gardner published a book titled *Frames of Mind*, which theorized that people learn and process information through seven different types of learning styles or intelligences (linguistic, logic-mathematical, musical, spatial, bodily kinesthetic, interpersonal, and intrapersonal). In 1999 he added an eighth intelligence, labeled naturalist.

Chapter 1

Understanding Special Needs Education

A Look Back at Special Needs Education

Leading tours of our facilities for prospective families, we as educators become privy to so much information about families. From fears of their children getting "too much Judaism" or "not enough Hebrew" to the way that the parents interact (and even bicker!) with each other, the introduction process reveals much about the way a family ticks. Every so often, we come across a parent who takes us back through a window of time, revealing the ghosts of special education from the past.

Though many families join our congregations with a wide-ranging vision of what they want for their children, sometimes we meet parents with a limited view of how a synagogue can support their family's needs. Because students with special needs were not usually visible in the religious school or youth programs in their congregations growing up, parents often assume that today's programs are designed for typical learners only. An educator may still hear questions like these: "You think my child can learn how to read Hebrew?" or "You mean my child can become bar mitzvah?"

In the past, religious schools in congregations, like their weekday school counterparts, rarely addressed the issue of special needs in the regular classroom. Typically, parents of children with autism or cognitive impairment would keep their children at home while other siblings participated in group learning and activities at the synagogue. In other cases, parents would enroll children with less visible special needs in religious school without recognizing the need to tell educators about the child's particular needs or behaviors. Teachers were left to wonder why these children were not performing well in the classroom and would consider them difficult or unintelligent.

At weekday schools, children with special needs were separated and placed into special education classrooms. When it came time for bar or bat mitzvah, parents of these children may have asked their congregations for some type of ritual to mark their children's coming of age. Empathetic rabbis would then create a ceremony allowing for the child's brief participation.

Other congregations sometimes even offered special accommodations for a child's classroom participation when the parents were vocal about their child's needs. But, as a rule, little was done to create a long-range, holistic plan for children with special needs. Very few congregational schools, if any, had special resources for these children besides a Hebrew language lab or remedial teachers.

The Inclusion Movement

Inclusion is the philosophy that all types of learners can be educated in one environment or, more commonly, in a "regular classroom." Because inclusive education is still a relatively new approach, it can take on a number of different forms in practice. However, educators who believe in inclusion work to make accommodations so that all students are taught in the same classroom or classrooms.

Although there is no single, universal concept of inclusion and no legal definition of *inclusion* or *inclusive education*, many organizations and advocacy groups have developed their own definitions. *Inclusive education*, according to its most basic definition, means that students with special needs are supported in chronologically age-appropriate general education classes and receive specialized instruction spelled out in their individualized education programs (IEPs). Inclusion is an effort to make sure students with special needs go to school along with their friends and neighbors, while also receiving whatever "specially designed instruction and support" they need to achieve high standards and succeed as learners (Halvorsen and Neary 2001, page 59).

Inclusive education developed out of a progression of special education trends, beginning in the 1970s. First, students were moved from specialized institutions to special classrooms. Then resource rooms became the norm for special education students, followed by mainstreaming, and, finally, a push to place all special education students in general education classrooms. In 1975, Congress passed the Education of All Handicapped Children Act, which mandated that students must be educated in the "least restrictive environment." In response, schools began creating segregated learning centers in their buildings. However, the special needs students in these centers rarely interacted with their general education peers (Aylor, Garriott, and Synder 2001, 199).

In the 1980s, mainstreaming became the dominant trend. In this model, students with special needs were moved from self-contained classrooms to general education classrooms, as their academic and social skills improved. When these students did not function well in the general classroom, they were returned to the special education classroom (Aylor, Garriott, and Snyder, 2001, 199). Mainstreaming may be considered the first step toward inclusive education, yet it only integrated the students with less severe special needs with the rest of their classmates.

The real drive for inclusion began in the mid-1980s, when educators identified a "problem of creating specific programs for specific types of children without considering any interaction with other programs." (Aylor, Garriott, and Snyder 2001, 199). They petitioned the U.S. Office of Special Education and Rehabilitation Services, calling for general and special education educators to join together through the regular education initiative (REI). Through REI, general education classes began providing services for individual learners. Though this movement still did not take into consideration students with severe special needs, it served as a bridge between the mainstreaming and inclusion models (Aylor, Garriott, and Snyder 2001, 199).

Although the terms are often mistakenly used interchangeably, *inclusion* differs from *mainstreaming.* Mainstreaming attempts to move students from special education classrooms to regular education classrooms only in situations where they are able to keep up with their typically developing peers without specially designed instruction or support. It provides only "part-time" inclusion, preventing students from becoming full members of the classroom community. Inclusion advocates sought to go a step further, fully integrating typical learners and students with special needs into the same classrooms. This newer concept of inclusion developed due to the "lack of satisfactory academic performance by students with disabilities, combined with growing demands for social equity and civil rights, increasing identification of students requiring services, and ballooning cost of special education" (McLaughlin, Rea, and Walther-Thomas, 2002, page 56).

Though some question whether inclusion works, the majority of research concludes that it does. One study focused on verifying the impacts of inclusion on both students with special needs and their regular education peers. Results documented significant positive attitudinal and learning impacts of inclusion for those with special needs as well as their peers without special needs. The special needs students reported higher self-concept, positive views of school and teachers, and greater motivation to work and learn. Unexpectedly, the regular education student responses followed the same patterns, reflecting significantly higher attitudes across the board and perceived academic achievement, as well as higher tolerance for special needs students (Dupuis, http://www.naset.org/782.0.html).

Our goal as Jewish educators should be to meet these same objectives by allowing Jewish children with special needs to learn alongside their Jewish peers in Hebrew and Judaic studies classes. Specialized instruction outside the classroom, including special bar/bat mitzvah preparation, should also be part of our plans for these children. As we are learning from the secular education world, integrating special needs students into our classrooms will have a positive impact across the board—not only for the children with special needs, but for the other students and members of the larger community learning the lessons of tolerance and acceptance of all children.

A Call for Inclusion in Jewish Education

It was only after inclusion in the secular school world gained popularity in the late 1990s that several Jewish communities in North America began experimenting with resources for supplementary schools to address the education of students with special needs. In the spring of 2000, the Consortium for Special Educators in Central Agencies for Jewish Education (a subgroup of the Jewish Education Service of North America) began discussing the importance of bringing inclusion into day schools. At the time, there was also a limited effort by several Jewish communities with Jewish education bureaus, including Atlanta, Houston, and San Francisco, to provide grants for on-site specialists to work with teachers who had students with special needs in their synagogue classrooms. However, the role of that resource person was mainly to work on ways to teach these students Hebrew and overlooked the idea of creating a fully inclusive educational environment. So while these students may have been placed in typical classrooms, regular classroom teachers received little training and no individualized guidelines for the specific students. The special education department of the Jewish Education Center of Cleveland, by contrast, created a program in the mid-1990s that trained teens to provide one-on-one support for students with special needs in synagogue schools. (Goldstein and Levine 2000, 2–13).

In 2000, the Union of American Hebrew

Congregations (now the Union for Reform Judaism) published a resource, called *Al Pi Darco (According to Their Ways)*, containing educational materials for children with special needs in congregations. The goal of *Al Pi Darco* was "to help rabbis, religious school principals, teachers, teachers' aides, and families provide Jewish learning for students with disabilities" (Address and Hochman 2000, page 6). This booklet provided program suggestions, a plethora of hints for teaching students with special needs, and a snapshot of several congregations' programming.

Despite the great work that has been done in special education in the Jewish world, there are still few communities or synagogues offering a fully inclusive supplementary Jewish education program. With congregations and community educational agencies facing significant economic challenges, there has been little growth in inclusion programs over the past ten years. The obstacles, however, are as much philosophical as financial. Why? Because there is not yet a widespread understanding among educators and community leaders that advancing special needs education in supplementary schools serves all students better and helps build stronger communities.

Special Needs in Public Schools

In order to understand the work leaders in the Jewish community need to do to change the culture at congregational schools, it is important to understand what is going on in the public schools.

In general, there are two levels of intervention for students who qualify to have their special needs addressed in the public schools. On the first level, an action plan may be developed for a student who is initially referred by his or her parent or teacher as having health, academic, social/emotional, or behavior problems in the classroom. This is called a "504 plan" and takes its name from paragraph 504 of the Rehabilitation Act of 1973, which mandated classroom modifications for students with disabilities. With a 504 plan, the student does not receive direct therapy or instructional support from a certified special needs teacher. However, a school's team may provide classroom and testing modifications or other accommodations to help the student succeed in the classroom. The team of individuals who determine what can best help the student may be referred to by different names from state to state. In Georgia, this team is called the "Student Support Team." In New York, it is referred to as the "Child Study Team" at the elementary school level and the "Student Study Team" once students are in middle school. The team typically includes the student's parents, teachers, school psychologists, school counselors, speech-language pathologists, occupational therapists, and/or physical therapists. Who is involved in the team depends on the particular student's needs. The 504 plan will detail the student's needs and proposed accommodations and/or modifications. If a 504 plan is not created, since some students do not require specific classroom accommodations or modifications, the team may put together an action plan to best respond to the student's identified areas of need. This may include more individualized time with the teacher or assigning a teacher/tutor to help the child.

If the interventions set forth in the 504 plan are not successful after an appropriate amount of time, the team at the school level may decide to refer the student to a special education team. This means that the student will be referred for testing to further understand his or her special needs. Testing may include academic, social-emotional, cognitive, fine-motor, gross-motor, and/or speech-language evaluations. If the completed evaluation identifies an area in which the student qualifies for special needs services, then an individualized education program, or

IEP, is written. An IEP includes specific time intervals that the student will spend with a trained special educator. IEPs may allow for the student to spend the full day or portions of the day in a special needs classroom, while other parts of the day are spent in a general education classroom. IEPs are written for one full year and include specific goals and objectives that the student needs to accomplish within that year. An IEP also includes classroom and testing modifications for the teacher to implement.

Some parents of public school students choose to supplement the 504 plan or the IEP by calling on private, outside resources. Outside resources may include talk therapy with a counselor or psychologist, academic tutoring, speech-language therapy, occupational therapy, or physical therapy. Additionally, special needs resources vary from state to state. Parents in some states must advocate to get even the basic resources needed for their children. In cases like this, IEPs may not fully and accurately reflect the child's condition and his or her true needs.

Special Needs Services for Students in Private Schools

More and more private schools are successfully implementing the unique approaches to learning required by students with special needs. Programs are being created and developed with an inclusion mind-set and a range of models, structures, and services. The private school setting may allow children with special needs to work within a special program with a smaller teacher-to-student ratio or in a general education classroom alongside typically developing peers.

Some private schools are dedicated to specific special needs. These schools specialize in a variety of needs, including dyslexia, autism, attention-deficit/hyperactivity disorder, and other learning disabilities. Plans created for each student include individualized learning or behavioral goals and classroom accommodations. Students and teachers strive to achieve those goals throughout the day in all subjects and activities.

The newer trend of transition programs is also becoming popular in private schools. These programs offer children with special needs an intensive period of time to catch up with their peers and teach the child compensatory strategies to prepare them to transition into a regular educational setting. A transitional program allows for students to participate in nonacademic subjects, such as art, music, and physical education, with the rest of their grade.

Understanding the Language of Special Needs

Have you ever been in the midst of a conversation with other adults when those around you begin to discuss a topic foreign to you? Perhaps at a dinner party, for example, some of the guests get into a lively debate over the merits of a recent political reform of which you have little knowledge. You may smile, nod, and listen intently; however, you are unable to join in the conversation because you do not have any background on the issue. Jewish educators may have a similar feeling when they meet with a family and the parents begin to speak about their child who has a host of special needs.

As your congregation begins to welcome all types of learners into your religious school program, you will have parents who are open and eager to review the specifics of their child's special needs. This may include sharing IEPs, complex psychological reports, and other information. Without a grasp of some of the basic language of special needs, you may feel as if you are part of the dinner party conversation on a political reform with which you are unfamiliar. This section offers a guide to the basic lingo and vocabulary. You will develop an understanding of some of the most common types of special needs and various disabilities that may impact a child or children from a family of one of your congregants or prospective congregants. It will also help you feel more confident and at ease when opening a dialogue with parents about their child's needs. It is written in glossary style with basic definitions to assist you in understanding commonly used terms and diagnoses describing children with special needs. These definitions are not intended to be used to diagnose anyone in your congregation, but rather to assist you in understanding potentially unfamiliar terminology. Additionally, although examples of common behaviors are included with each of these definitions, when children exhibit these behaviors, it does not necessarily mean that they have this diagnosis.

Anxiety Disorders: A group of mental disorders characterized by feelings of acute anxiety, followed by ongoing fear. These feelings may cause physical symptoms, such as a sensation of the heart beating too fast or shakiness. Generalized anxiety disorder and obsessive-compulsive disorder are two of the more commonly seen in children.

- ***Generalized Anxiety Disorder (GAD):*** Children with GAD may worry excessively about a variety of things, such as grades, family issues, relationships with peers, and performance in sports. They tend to be overly hard on themselves, strive for perfection, and may frequently seek approval or reassurance from others. Examples of anxiety triggers may be a new classroom, a substitute teacher, or getting on a bus for a field trip.
- ***Obsessive-Compulsive Disorder (OCD):*** OCD is characterized by unwanted and intrusive thoughts (obsessions) and feeling compelled to repeatedly perform rituals and routines (compulsions) to try to ease anxiety. The obsessions may often cause emotional distress and extreme frustration for children. Individuals with OCD may feel the need to check things frequently, be plagued by repetitive and distracting thoughts, or perform routines and rituals over and over. Examples may be asking the same question repeatedly, frequent hand washing, or constantly rearranging books, papers, and supplies on their desks.

Attention-Deficit/Hyperactivity Disorder (ADHD): Children with ADHD have one or more of the following symptoms, which first occur before the age of seven: inattention, distractibility, impulsivity, and hyperactivity. There are three subtypes, each with its own pattern of behaviors:

- ***Inattentive Type:*** Students with inattentive ADHD have difficulty paying attention to details, maintaining sustained attention, and listening to and following instructions. They tend to be disorganized, distractible, and forgetful.
  EXAMPLE: While the teacher is talking, Josh is staring at the Sukkot decorations on the bulletin board, and he is listening to the noise in the hallway as another class is walking to the library.
- ***Hyperactive-Impulsive Type:*** Students with hyperactive-impulsive ADHD fidget and squirm; they have difficulty remaining seated, playing quietly, waiting their turn, and/or waiting in line; they run around, play, and/or talk excessively; they interrupt frequently; they always seem to be on the go; and they may blurt out an answer before a teacher finishes asking a question.
  EXAMPLE: Jacob keeps yelling out questions without raising his hand.
- ***Combined Type:*** Combined-type ADHD is the most common form of the disorder; it involves a combination of inattentive type and hyperactive-impulsive type ADHD.

EXAMPLE: Michael is always squirming in his seat and playing with things on his desk while the rest of the third graders are sitting quietly, listening to the teacher.

Auditory Processing Disorder (APD): Students with APD have difficulty making sense of the words they hear. Individuals with APD typically have difficulty distinguishing between similar sounds or words, and they have trouble hearing speech if background noise competes with what someone is saying. This is also commonly known as central auditory processing disorder (CAPD).
EXAMPLE: The frustrated teacher repeats three times for Johnny to turn to page 52 and subsequently yells at him for not paying attention.

Developmental Disabilities: A generic term referring to individuals who have significant cognitive limitations due to mental and/or physical impairments. People with developmental disabilities have problems with major life activities, including language, gross- and fine-motor skills, learning, self-help, and overall independent living.

Developmentally Delayed: A term used primarily by administrators of preschool programs and early intervention services to refer to children who are found to be delayed by 25 percent of their chronological age in one or more developmental areas, including cognition, use of language or speech, and physical, social or emotional, and self-help skills.

- Students with **intellectual delays** have difficulty learning at the same rate as their peers.
  EXAMPLE: The teacher is trying to teach Susie that the letter *bet* sounds like *B*. She has gone over it with her multiple times. Once she begins teaching the next letter, *vet*, Susie already forgets what sound a *bet* makes.
- Students with **speech or language delays** may have trouble verbalizing certain sounds, making their speech hard to understand, or they may have difficulty expressing what they want to say because they have a limited vocabulary.
  EXAMPLE: Chelsea, who has cerebral palsy, cannot pronounce many of the big words in *V'ahavta* because she cannot enunciate the sounds.
- Students with **physical delays** may have gross-motor delays, meaning they cannot walk well or they may have to use a wheelchair. Students with fine-motor skill delays may have difficulty writing, holding a fork or spoon, or cutting with scissors. *Example*: Jonathan cannot complete an art project because of his inability to hold scissors.
- Students with **social/emotional delays** may be socially immature, compared to the other children in their class, and they will subsequently have difficulty making friends or even just initiating a conversation with a peer.
  EXAMPLE: Lori always sits by herself during break time, while the other kids laugh and talk about the latest TV show or movie.
- Students with **delays in the self-help area** have difficulty taking care of themselves.
  EXAMPLE: Ashley needs help taking off her pants so she can go the bathroom.

Dysgraphia: A learning disability resulting from the difficulty in expressing thoughts in writing and graphing.
EXAMPLE: When David is writing, he has difficulty writing in a straight line, and he frequently mixes up letters.

Dyslexia: A learning disorder marked by impairment of the ability to recognize and comprehend written words.
EXAMPLE: When Alex is reading Hebrew, he complains that the words look as though they are moving on the page.

Giftedness: Though there are no nationally recognized or even statewide guidelines used to define *giftedness*, it is usually characterized by children with high IQ scores. Keep in mind that so-called "gifted" children may exhibit behaviors resembling those of a child with ADHD.

Hearing Impaired/Hard of Hearing/Deafness: An impaired ability or a complete inability to process linguistic information through hearing.

Mildly Intellectually Disabled (MID)/Moderately Intellectually Disabled (MOID)/Severely Intellectually Disabled (SID): Terms used by public school systems to describe children with significant learning delays and below-normal IQ scores.

- Students with a **mild intellectual disability** have below-average intelligence, resulting in academic and social delays.
  EXAMPLE: Other children leave Brian out during free time because he "looks and acts different."
- Students with a **moderate intellectual disability** have significantly impaired intelligence, resulting in academic, motor, and social delays. This is often associated with another disability.
  EXAMPLE: Ten-year-old Susan has Down syndrome and has the social interests and language skills of a four-year-old.
- Oftentimes, students with a **severe intellectual disability** are nonverbal and have significant physical impairments. This is often associated with another disability.
  EXAMPLE: Jason uses a wheelchair and does not speak.

Nonverbal Learning Disability (or Disorder) (NVLD): NVLD is similar to Asperger syndrome, but it is generally considered milder than Asperger's. Students with NVLD have difficulty interpreting nonverbal social cues, such as gestures, body language, and tone of voice. They generally also have difficulty with coordination and balance problems, difficulty with spatial orientation, and sensory issues.
EXAMPLE: While Ryan is an excellent Hebrew reader, he speaks in an odd voice, does not look Mrs. Rosenberg in the eye, and will only speak with his classmates about golf, his favorite sport.

Perceptual Problems: Children with perceptual problems have difficulty perceiving and processing sensory information, including sound, taste, and touch. Examples include having difficulty with visual discrimination (discerning subtle differences in visual information, such as the differences between a printed *resh* and a *dalet* in Hebrew), visual memory, auditory discrimination (the child hears the letter *mem* as *nun*), following oral directions, and visual motor skills (these may include having difficulty doing art projects or writing).

Pervasive Developmental Disorders (PDDs): A group of disorders characterized by delays in the development of socialization and communication skills. Autism is the most thoroughly studied PDD; others include Asperger syndrome, childhood disintegrative disorder, and Rett syndrome.

- ***Autism:*** Children with autism have difficulties with social interaction and communicating with their peers. They may exhibit behaviors referred to as "stimming"—repetitive body movements that self-stimulate one or more senses in a regulated manner. They also tend to have a limited range of activities and interests.
  EXAMPLE: Eric, a high-functioning child with autism, flaps his hands often during class and likes to tell everyone all the details about *Star Wars*.

- ***Asperger Syndrome:***[1] A neurological condition characterized by normal intelligence and language development, but autistic-like behaviors and marked deficiencies in social and communication skills.
  EXAMPLE: Avi looks down whenever answering questions in class.
- ***Childhood Disintegrative Disorder (CDD):*** Children with CDD develop a condition that resembles autism but only after a relatively prolonged period (usually two to four years) of normal development.
  EXAMPLE: Three-year-old Kevin stopped talking.
- ***Rett Syndrome (RS):*** RS is a distinctive neurodevelopmental disorder that begins to show its effects in infancy or early childhood. Apraxia, the inability to perform motor movements, including eye gaze and speech, is the most fundamental and the most severely handicapping aspect of RS. Dyspraxia, the reduced ability to carry out these functions, characterizes those with milder cases of RS. Unlike all the above types of PDDs, which are more common in males, RS is seen almost exclusively in females, although it can occur in boys in rare cases.
  EXAMPLE: Sarah is unable to talk.

Receptive Language Disorder/Language Processing Disorder: Terms referring to a learning disorder characterized by difficulty understanding what is said. Children with receptive language disorder hear and process the sounds in words but have difficulty processing meaningful information, especially when the language is complex.
EXAMPLE: Jonathan's teacher asks him to turn to page 3 and read line 5, and Jonathan turns to page 5 and does not say anything.

Sensory Integration (SI) Issues: Difficulty processing everyday sensations, such as touch, taste, and sound. Children with SI issues may also exhibit unusual behaviors: They might avoid or, conversely, seek out opportunities to touch or move, hear particular sounds, and see certain sights.
EXAMPLE: Evan becomes abnormally scared during a fire drill.

Specific Learning Disability (SLD): Those with SLD have difficulty grasping spoken or written language and lag behind in nonverbal skills. The term is used by some public school systems instead of terms like dyslexia or dysgraphia. A child with an SLD demonstrates a discrepancy between intellectual ability and achievement levels in one or more of the following areas: oral expression, listening comprehension, written expression, basic reading skills, and mathematical calculation and reasoning.
EXAMPLE: Maggie has difficulty formulating her thoughts and she keeps using the wrong words when she is telling the class what she did for the Passover holiday.

Specific Reading Disability/Developmental Phonological Disorder: Delays in phonological awareness (understanding that sentences are composed of words, words are composed of sounds, and so on). Children with these disorders have difficulty dividing words into syllables or phonemes (sounds) and blending sounds together, especially when reading unfamiliar words. This is a common symptom of dyslexia (see above).

1 While the term *Asperger's* will probably be used for years to come, in December 2012 the American Psychiatric Association announced it will remove the term from its latest edition of the *Diagnostic and Statistical Manual of Mental Disorders.*

Tourette Syndrome: Tourette syndrome is a neurological disorder that causes tics. These are unwanted twitches, movements, or sounds that people make. Though children may have tics without having Tourette syndrome, children are only diagnosed when they have two tics that affect body movement and one that is a sound (all observed over at least one year). Although children with Tourette syndrome may seem disrespectful, these tics are involuntary and may include inappropriate language or curse words.

While this list briefly outlines typical behaviors and effects of the majority of special needs you may encounter, each student may exhibit different specific behaviors and difficulties. In addition, many special needs may overlap, causing even more difficulty in recognizing them. Because of the complexity of each special need, educators must rely on diagnoses from psychologists, psychiatrists, and speech, language, and development professionals, and should not attempt to label or diagnose students simply based on their behaviors and deficiencies. A list of additional resources appears in Appendix A.

Chapter 2

Building an Inclusive Program

What Does Change Look Like?

To keep up with the secular educational world, synagogues need to make changes in the way we approach special needs. Although change can alter the way something looks or feels, it does not always have to be difficult or drastic to make a profound difference. As educators, clergy, or congregational leaders, we have all introduced changes, whether big or small, into our congregations and programs. Some of those changes went smoothly, while others were more difficult to implement. As with Newton's Third Law of Motion, we realize that every action (or change) causes some type of reaction. Planning for the reactions and proper communications during the process typically eases the transition through the change.

In congregational education, the most profound change we can make is in our language. Not only should we choose terminology that welcomes differences and reduces the stigma associated with special needs, but when special needs are involved we should also get into the habit of starting with the word *yes* (even before we have a complete plan for implementation). While some parents of children with special needs are positive and forthcoming, others may seem demanding or even abrasive. When we come across these parents, it is important to remember that their reactions may be a product of their history of negative experiences with other educational organizations and institutions.

Most of their career (and, for many parents, advocating for their children becomes as much work as a full-time job), they have confronted the word *no*. Though generally said to them in an empathetic manner, they come to expect the ultimate answer to be negative. Beginning with the word *yes* (and being careful not to follow it with *but*) opens up the possibility of a partnership. Consider responding to parents with an answer like this: "Of course . . . Now let's begin discussing how we can work together to make this happen." This is a promising opening that does not commit to accommodations happening immediately.

A couple of weeks after the beginning of the

school year, a new family moved to Atlanta with three children, the middle child being a child with autism. During their synagogue shopping, they were greeted with a mixed bag of responses. When we met the family, we immediately told them about our program for students with special needs. They were shocked by the fact that their son's needs did not scare us away. We gave them the option of starting their older and younger children immediately and asked them for a couple of weeks to find a shadow for their son with autism. The welcoming nature of the first conversation opened up a partnership with the family and the parents responded, "Please take all the time that you need. We are just overjoyed that our son will be welcomed into a religious school."

The second language change occurs in the terminology used to present your program and to address students' needs. Phrases such as *remedial instruction*, *behavioral needs*, and *special needs teachers* isolate those who learn differently and add stigmas to their challenges. These phrases can be replaced by *learning support*, *positive reinforcement plans*, and *learning consultants*. It is also important to always name the child first, instead of the special need or disorder—a "child with autism" or a "child who learns differently," not an "autistic child" or a "special needs child." Because there is no single best vocabulary for special needs, in your educational teams (of professionals and lay leaders) we suggest that you create language appropriate for your program. The most important aspect is listening to all language and evaluating it to be sure that it does not isolate or stigmatize. In our congregation, our staff adopted the term *learning difference*.

Paralleling a reconsideration of language, we advise another major change, involving how your congregation advocates for those with differences. Beginning with the clergy and the professional staff, an effort should be made to educate your congregation about the philosophy of inclusion. At educational committees and faculty meetings, conversations should focus on the importance of leveling the playing field for all congregants. Sharing powerful stories, such as "Welcome to Holland" by Emily Perl Kingsley (Appendix B, page 113), and brainstorming ways to make your school or congregation more accessible to those who learn differently, are great ways to create buy-in among interest groups. Committee members, teachers, or clergy should then take a few weeks following these conversations to digest the ideas before implementing the next steps.

It is most important to know that change does not need to take place overnight and steps toward a new model can be taken with little or no cost. In our congregation, this cultural change took almost ten years, and we continuously work to modify and improve our program. Setting some simple goals for the semester or year, such as providing a professional development workshop on understanding special needs,[1] meeting with a handful of parents about assisting their children with a couple of simple accommodations, and meeting with clergy or other leaders, are the first steps toward congregational change.

As you move forward with your cultural change, there is one important additional point to bear in mind about this process. As with any change, you are going to need allies and assistance. Though you may not be instituting major changes at first, keep on the lookout for financial and physical resources for the future. Lay leaders and educators should start by checking with local Jewish Federations (or those in nearby larger communities for congregations in smaller cities), Jewish Family Service organizations, or other Jewish foundations for grant offerings or program assistance. Rabbis and educators should also seek out potential donors to endow a pro-

2 The National Dissemination Center for Children with Disabilities has numerous suggestions for finding training workshops in your area (http://nichcy.org/schools-administrators/staffdevelopment#start). Within your community, you may also be able to call on educational psychologists and special needs professionals to present workshops on special needs to teachers free of charge.

gram or start a fund for the congregation, earmarked for the special needs program. In addition, speak to local principals and parents to create a database of effective educational psychologists and psychiatrists, speech-language pathologists, occupational therapists, special education teachers, American Sign Language (ASL) interpreters, and other professionals who will give you advice throughout the process. Even if your congregation is not yet ready for such substantial change, keep a listing of resources to support your needs as they arise.

Making Your School and Congregation Welcoming to All

As educators, we find ourselves so concerned about the first day of school. Will the bulletin boards be completed? Are all teachers preparing engaging, get-to-know-you activities? Have they all prepared a letter to go home, explaining their plans for the year? Clearly, first impressions make all the difference for a program. We know that if parents walk in and see an organized learning structure with welcoming teachers and classrooms, they will have a positive attitude and will be serious about their commitment to the supplemental school. On the flip side, if they see a disorganized learning environment with second-rate teachers and little or no curriculum, they will think of the program as a glorified form of babysitting. When we create expectations for a successful year for "typical students," we often overlook the families of children with special needs.

Just as we spend time preparing our teachers and our classrooms for the opening of the school year, we should begin critically examining how congregational buildings look and feel to families whose children have learning or physical challenges. This begins with handicapped accessibility. In newer buildings, architects have taken care of these standards by law. Sinks and door handles are at the proper height, ramps and elevators are next to stairs, and signage designates how to access particular areas in a wheelchair. In older structures, however, much work may need to be done. If you have an architect or contractor in your congregation, he or she would be a good resource when it comes to accessibility issues. Walk through your building together and create an inventory of items that do not meet the requirements of the Americans with Disabilities Act of 1990. Though you may not have the funds to fix most of them, once you have pinpointed the issues, there may be creative ways around them to accommodate all learners.[2] In literature distributed to parents about the religious school, it is a good idea to stress that the school will do its best to make appropriate physical and educational accommodations for students with special needs. You might also add that if parents have concerns about particular physical aspects of the building that may influence their child's learning, they should share those concerns with the director of education or the learning consultant.

In addition to determining the problematic issues in your building, you should also work to camouflage programs and resources that assist students with special needs. Ultimately, if people were to walk into a classroom in your religious school, it should be difficult for them to determine if any students had special accommodations. In other words, the ideal classroom has a teacher implementing most of the strategies designed for special needs in all of his or her teaching. For example, when a teacher tells her students to turn to page 50 in their workbooks, he or she should also write *page 50* on the board. This will enable students who have auditory processing needs to follow the teacher's instruction. Also, it is important to have students learning with classroom assistants seated in the main seating area and not in a corner of the room. Part of the suggested faculty

3 The Union for Reform Judaism offers information on low-cost alternatives to make accommodations in your congregation, as well as many other valuable resources. Contact the URJ at 855-URJ-1800 or urj1800@urj.org for more information.

training in Appendix D includes sensitivity training exercises and teaching strategies to assist all learning styles in the classroom.

Bringing the Faculty and Clergy Onboard

To create a successful inclusion plan for your school, it is crucial to address any negative preconceived feelings among faculty and staff about educating all students in the classroom. Inclusive education is a relatively new approach (becoming common only in the last ten to twenty years), and many teachers will have spent little if any time working with students with special needs, especially those with limited experience in secular education settings. There is a natural fear that comes with teaching nontraditional students. Many teachers may even feel that reaching out to students with special needs will create unwanted issues in their classrooms. So before making any major changes, work to create a sense of cohesion on the subject. Even when everyone seems to be onboard, you will find that certain teachers never really "get it" and that new fears will develop among staff members, even years after your program has proven successful.

Facilitating staff training workshops on inclusion is key. As you plan a faculty workshop, consider inviting your clergyperson and education committee chair to participate. Workshops should be designed not only to teach the necessary skills for working with students with special needs, but also to generate empathy and awareness among participants. The ultimate goal of the training session is to create partners. Even if teachers and clergy members do not master the techniques, buy-in among stakeholders is the true measure of success. This will open the door for future professionals and lay leaders working in your school to do the critical work. Soon you will find your rabbi or cantor coming to these leaders for direction as they prepare a child to become bar or bat mitzvah. And, along with that trust, your teachers will develop a new sense of happiness in their classrooms, knowing that they are not working alone.

Setting the Mission and Scope of the Program

As your congregational school begins to develop a plan for inclusion, the education director and the education committee should work together to decide what role the educator will play in the plan and who will fill other key roles. The educator, with or without the assistance of the lay committee or clergyperson, can then begin to develop a plan for the first steps of inclusion. This plan may be as simple as setting concrete goals for year one and preliminary goals for year two. The goals should take into account the "who," "what," "where," "when," "how," and "why" of the initial steps. At a minimum, the educator should be part of all decisions and review and approve all accommodations made for students in the school.

The educator is the center of all preliminary inclusion planning, but as a holistic plan for inclusion in the school begins to develop, a dedicated facilitator should be secured. This facilitator, who will be referred to as the "learning consultant," will oversee all programmatic aspects of an inclusion plan and will partner with the educator. The learning consultant does not need to be an employee of the congregation, though that's advisable. Jewish special needs educators, doctors, therapists, or other special needs professionals often enjoy helping children in a religious setting and may benefit from additional income. The salary of the position will depend on the number of students served and the number of hours the learning consultant is expected in the classroom. Even after the learning consultant is brought on, the role of the educator will remain to meet with families and do the initial intake, explain the school's inclusive philosophy and the process for implementing accommodations, work with teachers to implement classroom modifications, stay informed of the students' progress as they advance, and make decisions, in conjunction with the clergyperson and the learning consultant, that promote the success of each student. The educator and learning consultant will work in partnership to recruit teenagers to volunteer as special needs classroom assistants, who will be referred to as *tzadikim*;[3] plan and possibly facilitate workshops for those working with special needs students; and provide resources as needed for a developing program in the religious school.

The role of a learning consultant may be different in each congregation. He or she does not need to be present at every Hebrew or religious school session. Regular campus visits provide adequate coverage as the congregational educator may serve as the day-to-day liaison for *tzadikim*. In larger congregations with a larger number of students with special needs, and with multiple school days and school locations, the position of learning lab coordinator should be considered. The learning lab coordinator should be present each school day to monitor coverage and coordinate the scheduling of students. The coordinator does not need to have a background in special needs. He or she can be a compassionate Hebrew teacher who has gone through an inclusive education training program.

The learning consultant (as opposed to the learning lab coordinator) should have a solid background in special education; however, he or she does not need to have extensive knowledge of Hebrew.[4] The main role of the learning consultant is to develop learning plans for all students (see chapter 3), to evaluate and record student progress, to train *tzadikim*, and to meet or be in contact with parents periodically to update learning plans. The learning consultant also serves as the advisor to educators and clergy on all special needs accommodations.

The educator and the learning consultant must also make decisions about the structure of a learning lab. A learning lab should be a relatively quiet space (or multiple spaces) where the educator, the learning lab coordinator or the learning consultant, and *tzadikim* can sit down with students at a table or desk to work individually on Hebrew phonics, reading, or prayers, using multisensory strategies and positive reinforcement. The lab does not necessarily need to be in one designated space, but must be a place with relatively little noise and few distractions. Some schools may find that nooks within the classrooms or library serve this purpose well. If you don't have one designated lab, a central supply closet or area should be set up with necessary learning aids (such as highlighters, enlarged copies of prayers, and multisensory learning tools, like modeling clay, bendable wax sticks, and pipe cleaners) and a private place for the learning consultant or learning lab coordinator to post schedules and keep learning plans or private information about students.

During the initial implementation of a plan or program, don't get too bogged down by the titles and players. As explained earlier, a solid inclusive learning program develops slowly over time. At first, because the school will implement only minimal changes and accommodations, the educator may serve all the required roles. This book, in combination with the training guide for *tdikim*, provides all the necessary training to implement a special needs program.

4 This term is fully described in chapter 4. Many congregations refer to teenage volunteers as *madrichim*, which means "guides" in Hebrew. We use *tzadikim*, Hebrew for "righteous ones," in recognition of the special role and training required of *madrichim* working with students with special needs.

5 The learning consultant should be proficient in Hebrew reading, however.

Accommodation Teams

Even if your school is just beginning to create an inclusive environment, be sure to set up a process to review proposed accommodations for students and put them in place. Typically, the process for implementing all accommodations begins with the educator. Whether the request comes from a parent, a teacher, a clergyperson, or the learning consultant, it is important for the educator to be the first point of contact and the gatekeeper for change. Schools should work to avoid a situation where separate conversations are held between teachers, parents, and clergy, and these conversations are not documented as part of a holistic plan for the student. Though each student may have his or her own unique plan each year, the overall accommodations should be devised as part of a larger system, where the accommodations advance with the child throughout the program.

Accommodation teams typically consist of the educator and the learning consultant; however, some schools may choose to add additional members to these teams. A physician, a psychologist, a psychiatrist, a social worker, a speech-language pathologist, and/or a special needs teacher would all be appropriate additions to the team. Even if they are not on the accommodation team itself, it is crucial to compile a list of these professional resources to consult with, should a situation arise that is beyond the expertise of the team members. In our congregation, a teacher was asked by parents on the first day of school to administer an emergency medical procedure, as needed, for a student who has had a history of medical issues. Though it was our intention to provide the best care for the student during school hours, two local pediatricians advised against having the teacher perform the procedure for multiple reasons. At that point, citing the advice of the physicians, we went back to the parents to create a new emergency plan for that student, with the parents on call to administer the procedure themselves.

A key role of the accommodation team is to create easy-to-implement and low-cost plans for students before they enter the classroom. Because of their overall understanding of the building and the student's needs, these teams can reassign learning spaces as needed. For example, if a student has impaired walking abilities or is in a wheelchair, and the building does not have full handicap accessibility, a simple accommodation would be to reassign that particular student's class to a ground-level classroom or space. Along with that change, the team would put together a plan to assist the teacher with furnishing or space requirements so he or she can focus on teaching rather than problem solving. During the planning, the team should schedule a meeting with the teacher or teachers to elicit any necessary input to make the accommodation smoother for the teacher and student.

Another example of a creative accommodation for students deals with emergency drills. Oftentimes, students with special needs are confronted with sensory issues or anxiety from sudden transitions. Though schools need to conduct unannounced emergency drills, the learning consultant should set up a plan for students with special needs during these drills. Before every emergency drill at our school, we have a communication plan in place with our *tzadikim* and our learning lab coordinator. Once we let them know about an upcoming drill, they set the plan in place to evacuate certain students just prior to the exercise. Along with this plan, they practice evacuations at off times for these students without the stress of loud bells or sirens and large crowds.

Strategic Program Evaluation

As you put your program into action, remember that not every intervention will be an immediate success. Because there is no one-size-fits-all solution to educating students with special needs, educators and parents should expect a period of trial and error. A procedure for regularly evaluating a student's progress should be part of every plan. Constant communication with teachers is key. When teachers report difficulties over several weeks, a new plan must be put in place. Conversely, a smooth-running classroom is evidence of a successful plan. *Tzadikim* should be consulted regularly regarding the successes and challenges of the students with whom they are working. Even with the best accommodations, sometimes a child does not succeed in the classroom. Some children have such complex needs that professional assistance is required to include them. In these cases, the educator and learning consultant should work in partnership with the parents to find additional funding for a paid, professionally trained facilitator, if the parents cannot afford it themselves. These facilitators have extensive training in classroom intervention techniques and special education. Discretionary funds from the clergy, grants, and donations can also be sought to offset the expense.

The evaluation plan should also include a meeting or communication with parents before the beginning of the school year and at the end of each school year. During that meeting, the learning consultant should gather medical or psychological updates on the student, and the current plan should be reviewed. Oftentimes, the parents can see progress or failures that teachers and *tzadikim*, who typically only interact with students once or twice a week, may miss.

Another evaluation should come from the learning consultant and/or the learning lab coordinator, who makes use of tools, such as checklists, for Hebrew learning. A file should be kept for each student in the learning lab and updated regularly.

Staff Training for Classroom Teachers

Once a philosophy of inclusive education has been adopted by congregational leadership, the next step is to bring the faculty onboard. Formal teacher training provides both a general understanding of inclusive education and practical tools for implementing this approach in the classroom.

Initial training sessions may be as short as one hour, but they should offer participants at least one new strategy or modification that can be implemented immediately by any teacher in any classroom. A good introductory staff training will include four elements:

1. empathy-building activities (used primarily as a set induction)
2. a discussion of the goals and scope of the program or change
3. a simple lesson on the most common special needs
4. a description of the process of implementation.

If a school does not have enough time or resources to train all teachers fully, the *tzadikim* curriculum can be used or adapted for training both high school students and adults together. Some congregations have found it valuable to invite adult teachers to the first *tzadikim* training workshop (approximately three hours, covering the first three chapters of the guidebook) before the school year begins. While teachers are encouraged to attend this intensive training, learning coordinators or educators should meet regularly with all teachers each year to discuss students with special needs and the ongoing role of the learning consultant. Additionally, each year the learning consultant should meet with new teachers separately to provide them with an understanding of the school's approach to students with special needs. Hebrew teachers will also require additional training to help them implement strategies and tools for multisensory Hebrew instruction in their classrooms.

We recommend beginning a training program with a meaningful and touching set induction or story. Two of our favorite stories are

Emily Perl Kingsley's "Welcome to Holland" and "Benjamin" from *Chicken Soup for the Teacher's Soul* (both reprinted with permission in Appendix B, page 113). A good opening story touches the heartstrings of the listener and helps promote a desire for change in the classroom. In addition to stories, you should use empathy-building exercises, such as a blindfolded trust walk. The *tzadikim* guide includes several user-friendly exercises for creating an understanding of specific special needs.

Once your teachers and staff have been emotionally charged through a set induction, clear and simple goals should be briefly outlined. Rather than presenting a long list of generic aims, the presenter should create a short list of no more than five specific goals that reflect the congregation's or school's character. For instance, if your school is family-oriented, one goal might be to provide large-print prayer packets for family services to students with special needs. In a program known for its success with informal education, a goal might be to provide *tzadikim* for students with special needs at youth group events or to develop activities and games that promote equality and celebrate differences. Each goal should be followed by specific examples of how teachers can help meet the goals in their classrooms activities.

When presenting common special needs, the presenter should provide a simple definition of each one, followed by a specific example that accurately portrays the characteristics of the special need (see chapter 1). Care should be taken by the presenter to avoid alluding to specific students in the school. Caution teachers against attempting to diagnose students on the basis of simple definitions and examples, or to implement classroom modifications without a plan in place and the cooperation of parents and administrators.

Finally, the presentation should spotlight specific classroom modifications for teachers. Appendix F provides a list of examples of modifications described in the *tzadikim* guide. Since many of the techniques and philosophies may be new to staff members, it is not necessary to teach all methods in one workshop. Choose three to six modifications and spend adequate time on each one. Additional modifications can be introduced at monthly staff meetings or at a follow-up workshop later in the school year.

EXPENSES AND FUNDING

Focusing on Program Goals and Identifying Expenses

Commitment to a fully inclusive philosophy to educate all students in the same classroom setting and an organized structure led by a strong educational leader are more important to the success of a program than the size of the budget. Therefore, before creating and implementing a budget, the educator must be sure that faculty members and clergy are fully invested in this way of thinking. If the educational leaders (the clergy, the education committee, and any other school administrators) are not yet onboard, more work should be done to create buy-in among key stakeholders before moving forward with a program.

Once the educational leaders are onboard, the educator should carefully design an introductory budget. An inclusive program does not necessarily require additional funding to succeed. The scope of the program being created will dictate the extent of budget additions. However, with careful and creative spending, the program will add minimal expense to a congregation's budget.

Because inclusion is a relatively new concept to most congregations, start with a small budget that will not drastically alter religious school tuition. The idea of inclusion is for all families to be treated equally and parents of special needs students should not have to pay any additional costs. Therefore, program expenses should be included in the general school budget and all families should be reassured that an inclusive program barely affects school tuition. If the inclusion program's budget is so large that it will make an impact on the overall school budget, consider implementing incremental changes over several years. The goal at this point is to introduce the program in such a way that families become accustomed to it and see its positive impact. Introducing the program with a tuition increase may cause a backlash from parents who do not yet understand the importance of inclusion.

The primary expense for a special needs program is the learning consultant (if that is a paid position) and, if necessary, the learning lab coordinator. Many schools already have a remedial teacher or a reinforcement teacher on staff. If this is the case in your school, the educator should transition this teacher into the role of learning lab coordinator or change this position to that of learning lab coordinator. The salary should be in line with a beginning Hebrew teacher and the hours should be during regular school hours only. If a program includes both religious school on Sundays and Hebrew school during the week, the educator may choose to have the learning lab coordinator on site only one of the two meeting days. In programs with multiple midweek Hebrew school days or locations, it may be most economical for this person to be on site on Sunday mornings only, depending on the number of students served. Whether a program has a small or a large enrollment, there is no need to hire more than one learning lab coordinator, since the number of *tzadikim* working in the lab will increase with the size of the school (thus creating equal student-to-*tzadik(ah)* ratios).

Program supplies constitute the secondary expense of the program. These supplies include consumables (folders, binders, and copies for student records), manipulatives typically already included in a school supply budget (colored modeling dough, pipe cleaners, flash cards, highlighters, etc.), and photocopying expenses (for enlarging texts and making color copies for highlighted materials).

While some schools pay *madrichim* each week, it is not recommended to include a salary line for *tzadikim* as a program expense. More and more congregations are moving away from paying *madrichim*. The reason for this is twofold. First, many students need volunteer/community service hours to meet high school requirements or for state-funded college scholarships. If *madrichim* or *tzadikim* are paid, their hours do not technically qualify as volunteer hours. In addition, many educators have found that students working as volunteers take their job more seriously than students working for a minimal paycheck. When a congregation in Atlanta first eliminated *madrichim* salaries, the staff noticed an increase in enrollment and a stronger work ethic. When the *madrichim* were informally polled after the change, they shared comments like this: "When I was being paid, I felt that if I missed a day, I would just not receive a paycheck. However, when I work as a volunteer, I feel as if the school depends on me to be there." That congregation presents *madrichim* and *tzadikim* with gift cards from iTunes, Target, a bookstore, or the mall (usually a $100 gift card is presented to each postconfirmation volunteer and a small gift of around $10 to all preconfirmation volunteers) at the end of the year in lieu of a salary. Even though they are not paid, the Atlanta congregation has never had difficulty finding students to volunteer. If *tzadikim* are paid or a gift card will be presented to them at the end of the year, this should also be included in the budget planning. Additionally, keep in mind that with *tzadikim* in the classroom working individually with students with special needs, the number of other *madrichim* needed in the program will decrease (thus offsetting some of the *madrichim* expenses).

The final budget expense to be taken into account is the food and snacks for training sessions. It is recommended that you serve a meal at the first workshop. Consider budgeting for a more significant meal for the summer workshop and three smaller meals (like pizza) for the supplementary workshops. If a school has an active parent volunteer committee, lay-sponsored meals can reduce this budget line.

Remember that the real keys to a successful inclusion program are a congregational philosophy change, buy-in from faculty and clergy, a solid program structure, and proper support personnel (the learning consultant, lay leaders, *tzadikim*, psychologists, specialists, or special needs educators), and not the size of the budget. Even if the school had a staff of ten special needs teachers, without the proper leader directing the program and setting goals, the program would probably not be successful. When all staff members are onboard and are given direction by the learning consultant, the system produces successful results for all types of student learning styles.

One Final Note on Program Funding

As alluded to earlier, parents whose children are not or have not yet been diagnosed with special needs do not necessarily understand the importance of inclusion. Secular private schools typically charge families for special needs services, while public schools provide services for all students at no additional charge. Therefore, private school parents may expect families to pay for additional services at religious or Hebrew school, while public school parents may expect these services to be provided for free. Because most congregational schools include students from both public and private schools, it is important to find a happy medium between the two.

Ideally, a congregation should provide special needs services for students at no additional charge. However, when the idea of inclusion is brought up at an educational committee meeting, be prepared for a discussion about fears of adding fees to these families' tuition. Some education committees may not agree to include additional expenses in the greater education budget. It is also a good idea to involve the congregational rabbi in these discussions, as well as presenting persuasive stories from congregants about their children's needs and research from other congregations.

If, after the discussion, the education committee chooses to have participating families pay for these additional services, you might want to suggest charging a voluntary fee higher than the necessary cost to offset the cost for those who cannot pay the additional fee. Alternatively, you could try to find a donor who will cover the fees for these families. Since parents of children with special needs have so many specialist, therapist, and tutoring expenses, finances often prove challenging. This option will allow the program to generate the necessary income to support the budget, but will also assist those in need.

Chapter 3

Meeting Student Needs

How Do We Identify Students with Special Needs?

Identifying student needs is a multifaceted process and it often takes years to identify even half the students who would benefit from the special needs program. When starting the process, the educator must understand that many parents do not wish to share this information with a supplementary school and others do not realize that it can be beneficial to them. Because there is a stereotype that all Jewish children are intelligent, parents often feel that revealing a child's special needs will tarnish this reputation. Therefore, they may try to hide these needs from their friends and congregational communities. We should also remember that gifted children and those going through family challenges (like divorce or a family member's serious illness) may also need accommodations and should be included in the identification process as well.

The first step in recruiting students is creating awareness and promoting the program. In the early years of our inclusion model, we advertised the program by name (*Yad B'Yad, "Hand in Hand"*) so that it would sound like an established part of the school. Because it stood out by name in our program handbook, parents would often come forward to inquire about it. On tours of our congregation, we always make a concerted effort to share the success of this program with all parents, regardless of their children's needs, primarily to reduce the stigma of special needs. It is also important to introduce the program from the beginning of enrollment in religious school, so that if their children are diagnosed at some point in the future, parents will know that these resources are available.

The application or registration form is the second entrance point. While many congregations ask a lot of questions about special needs on these forms, we have found it most helpful to ask just a few questions and to do so in a noninvasive manner. Here's an example: "Does your child have any other special needs that might affect his/her learning experience in religious school (learning disabilities, giftedness, emotional issues, family issues, etc.)?" Sometimes, onerous forms keep parents from answering honestly. The educator or learning consultant must have a conversation or meeting with the parent anyway, where he or she will gather the necessary information. In the wording of the questions, it is crucial to give parents permission to schedule a meeting with the educator or learning consultant and to let them know that they may also be contacted by one of these professionals. Most important is to be clear that any information provided on the form is kept strictly confidential.

The third method for identifying students is in the classroom. Appendix C, see page 117, (a referral form) provides information about helping teachers identify signs of special needs in their classrooms. Recognizing the signs of special needs may sound relatively easy; however, students with needs often learn to overcompensate, and special needs are often interpreted as behavioral issues or students who seemingly "don't want to put in the effort." While a properly filled-out referral form is often helpful to the learning consultant, most supplementary school teachers do not have enough time to properly work through the process. Therefore, teachers should be reminded to e-mail or contact the educator and the learning consultant whenever they are concerned about a particular student in the classroom.

Once a student has been identified as having a possible need by a teacher or another faculty member, the educator or learning consultant must navigate carefully through the next phase. A typical first step is for the learning consultant and educator to observe the child. Next the educator will give the teacher permission to call the parent. The teacher must be careful not to insinuate that the child has a special need. During the teacher's conversation with the parent, the teacher should use statements and questions like, "Rebecca really has trouble sitting still during our class discussions. Do you have any suggestions for how I might help her in class?" or "I have noticed that Jonathan is having trouble reading out loud. Do you think his weekday teacher may have some suggestions so that I can be more sensitive to him?" These open-ended questions are designed to encourage the parent to divulge additional information about the student's learning style. If the parent shares that the child has a special need, the teacher should be ready to tell the parent about the school's learning consultant, who helps teachers work with students who learn differently. The teacher should ask the parent's permission for the learning consultant to contact him or her. In the reverse situation, where the parent is surprised by the news or does not acknowledge the need, the teacher just shares any information provided by the parent with the learning consultant, who documents the conversation. Though a diagnosis will not be made, the learning consultant can help the teacher identify strategies that may promote the child's learning.

Even with all these measures, you will likely not succeed in identifying all students with special needs. Therefore, it is critical to provide ongoing professional development for your teachers, so they understand how to teach all types of learners. We also reiterate to our teachers that everyone learns differently and almost everyone has different learning strengths and weaknesses. Even the best and most experienced teachers need to remind themselves to review lessons and classroom activities to be sure that they are accommodating all types of learners. The same procedures that are taught in the *tzadikim* training program should be implemented in all classrooms.

Understanding Individualized Education Programs and Psychological Reports

Though some families may try to hide their child's learning differences, or not deem it important to share with their congregational school, other families will be forthcoming, especially once they understand that your program welcomes all types of learners. In these scenarios, families may share various types of paperwork to help you understand their child's learning difference. In addition, once you discover that a child has a diagnosis, you should request these types of documentation to prepare a learning plan. To best utilize the critical information in these lengthy documents, you must first become familiar with both the critical and noncritical information contained in each document, and how this information can help you create an effective learning plan.

Understanding Special Education Eligibility Reports

Generally, a child who has an IEP will also have what is called a "special education eligibility report." The eligibility report explains and classifies the type of disability or disorder and why this is negatively impacting the child in the classroom. There are various categories of eligibility reports (such as for children with autism or speech-language impairments), and a child may have multiple reports. Most important, eligibility reports will have a statement at the end of the document stating whether the child qualifies as having the type of disability or delay for which he or she is being assessed. Eligibility reports vary in style and format from state to state, city to city, and county to county, and they may be handwritten or computer-generated.

Before writing an eligibility report, a psychologist, learning disability specialist, behavior specialist, speech-language pathologist, occupational therapist, and/or physical therapist will administer a variety of standardized and informal assessment measures, conduct interviews, and make classroom observations. These measures help to assess the child's level of functioning in a variety of areas. Since the terms vary from state to state, do not get hung up on the exact terminology. With practice, the content will be easy to identify, based on the following categories of diagnoses in eligibility reports by the public school system:

- ***Significantly Developmentally Delayed (SDD) or Developmentally Delayed (DD):*** This term is traditionally reserved for children in the prekindergarten or kindergarten age range. Once they are of school age, they are typically reassessed in order for the school district to more specifically classify their learning difference. Children with an SDD or DD eligibility report are assessed to see if they have an overall developmental delay in one or more areas.
- ***Autism or Autism-related:*** This diagnosis may include any of the PDDs defined in chapter 2, including high- or low-functioning autism or Asperger's. Children with this type of eligibility report are being assessed to see if they meet the criteria, and have one of the PDDs.
- ***Intellectual Disability (ID) or Mental Retardation (MR):*** These terms define whether a child has below-average IQ scores, or below-average intelligence, and how this impacts him or her academically. Children may be assessed as having a mild, moderate, or severe intellectual impairment.
- ***Learning Disability (LD) or Specific Learning Disability (SLD):*** This diagnosis is based on evaluating the child's full-scale IQ and his or her academic performance levels. If the examiner finds a discrepancy between the child's intelligence and his or her ability to perform academically up to his or her intellectual potential, the eligibility report may indicate that he or she qualifies as having a learning disability. Children may have learning disabilities in different areas, such as reading, writing, or math.

- ***Emotional/Behavioral Disorder (EBD):*** This is an assessment of social and emotional development, as well as how problem behaviors may negatively impact the child in the classroom setting and with the development of peer relationships.
- ***Speech-Language Disorder or Impairment (SLD/SLI):*** A speech-language pathologist administers a battery of speech-language tests and then determines if the child has significant speech disorders (characterized by the way the child's speech, voice, and articulation sounds, as well as the presence or absence of stuttering) and/or language disorders (characterized by the child's ability to understand and process what is being said to him or her and the child's ability to adequately use words and language to express him- or herself in the classroom setting).
- ***Other Health Impairments (OHIs):*** This is a catchall category for a variety of medical conditions, such as attention-deficit/hyperactivity disorder (ADHD), seizure disorder, or Tourette syndrome.

Secondary services may also be included in an eligibility report for a child with needs in one of the prior categories:

- ***Occupational Therapy Eligibility Report:*** A report written by an occupational therapist after assessing the child's fine-motor and sensory development and determining if he or she qualifies to receive occupational therapy as a related service to another one of the eligibility reports noted above.
- ***Physical Therapy Eligibility Report:*** A report written by a physical therapist after assessing the child's gross-motor development and determining if he or she qualifies to receive physical therapy as a related service to another one of the eligibility reports noted above.

All these eligibility reports will clearly state if the child meets the criteria of one or more of the diagnoses noted above. Looking at the very end of the report will very quickly let you know what type of disorder or disability a child has. Eligibility reports are completed every three years, so also pay close attention to the date of the eligibility report to know at what age the child was evaluated (more recent eligibility reports will have the most valuable and current information). Reading the eligibility report in its entirety, if it is a current report, can help you develop a thorough understanding of the child's strengths and weaknesses. These reports are typically brief and provide excellent information. Children with complex issues may have a more lengthy and detailed report. If this is the case, please review how to read a psychological report, detailed later in this chapter. If the report is not current, you should first glance at the qualifying diagnosis, and then use the child's IEP to better understand the child's current situation.

Understanding IEPs

If a child has an eligibility report stating that he or she has one of the disabilities or disorders noted above, the child will also typically have an IEP. Like eligibility reports, IEPs vary in style and format from place to place. The IEP contains information reiterating that the child qualifies to receive special education services as a result of meeting specific eligibility criteria, and the time, frequency, and duration of services provided, goals/objectives, and classroom accommodations.

What Part of the Document Should I Focus On?

There are certain parts of the IEP that are important to understand to best utilize the information and create a plan for the child's congregational school success. Other parts of the IEP are strictly related to the child's secular school and do not need to be read in detail. IEPs can be quite lengthy (some as long as thirty pages) so it is easy to feel overwhelmed. Instead of trying to read the IEP in its entirety, you may wish to skim through and review only the critical pieces of information contained within it. Here are the important parts of an IEP:

- ***The date of the IEP:*** This should be on the very front page of the IEP and will let you know how current the information is. IEPs stay current for a full calendar year in most school systems, yet some schools require a new IEP for each academic year. Even if the IEP you are reading is not current, it will still be helpful.
- ***The diagnosis:*** This typically appears at the beginning of the IEP and it will use the diagnosis from the child's eligibility report. On some IEPs, all possible diagnoses are listed in one area toward the beginning of the IEP and a check mark is placed next to those diagnoses for which the child is receiving services.
- ***Current level of performance:*** All IEPs contain a section in which the child's current levels of performance are detailed. This section is especially important if the paperwork you are reviewing does not include an updated eligibility report. Although it will not be as detailed as the information provided in an eligibility report, this section will include an assessment of the child's strengths and weaknesses that is helpful in allowing the teacher to best understand this child's capabilities and needs.
- ***The frequency and duration of services:*** The IEP will detail how many hours a week the child spends in a special education classroom or is receiving special education services. There are thirty hours in a typical school week, and if a child is spending the majority of his or her time in a special education classroom, this child will most likely need a *tzadik* or *tzadikah* in your congregational school. These students usually require a smaller teacher-to-student ratio, as well as multiple strategies to be successful in a congregational school.
- ***Classroom modifications and accommodations:*** This section includes specific strategies that the child's teachers use in the weekday school. These strategies should be shared with the child's congregational school teacher, ideally as part of the development of a learning plan (which will be discussed later in this chapter). A copy of this page should be shared with the teacher instead of the full IEP.

Students attending private schools may not have an IEP, but many will have had a full educational/psychological report (sometimes referred to as a psycho-educational report) completed, and the parents may choose to share this with you. Like an IEP, this report can also appear extensive and overwhelming, but by focusing on the following key elements of the report, you can gain a better understanding of the child's strengths and weaknesses, as well as how the child can learn best in an educational setting.

- ***Background information:*** Most psychological reports include an extensive amount of background information that will typically encompass a mapping of family dynamics, including developmental and social history, based on the psychologist's assessment of the child prior to testing.
- ***IQ testing:*** A full psycho-educational report will include the results of IQ testing. The Wechsler Intelligence Scale for Children is most commonly used to assess IQ. The results of the child's full-scale IQ test can give you a quick

understanding of the child's intellectual capacity, although, clearly, IQ alone is not enough to truly understand a child's strengths and weaknesses. Children with an IQ of over 130 are considered to be in the "very superior" intelligence classification, or more commonly known as "gifted." IQ scores between 90 and 120 are classified as "normal" and scores between 90 and 70 begin classifications from "dull normal" to "borderline." Children with scores below 70 have intellectual disabilities that may profoundly affect their learning capabilities. Though you shouldn't spend too much time analyzing IQ scores, keep in mind that some students with extremely high IQ scores may be confused with students with ADHD because they may get bored easily with basic learning and their minds will often wander to other more intellectually stimulating interests.

- ***Results and summary section:*** This section should include a summary of the testing results as well as a diagnosis that best fits the child.
- ***Classroom modifications:*** This section includes the psychologist's recommendations regarding what classroom strategies may be most beneficial. Oftentimes, this is found in the Recommendations section of the report.

Where Do I Go for Additional Assistance in Understanding the Terminology?

While this chapter should help you interpret a wide array of paperwork that may be provided for you or simply help you to better understand the children with special needs you may be including in your congregational school, it does not give you all the answers. Every child with special needs is unique and has his or her own complex profile and strengths and weaknesses. Do not hesitate to seek out additional resources to help you better understand how to include all children in your school's educational program. This may involve speaking to congregants who work in a related field or asking the parent of a student to connect you with the specialists with whom the child works. You will find that these specialists are already very invested in helping the child succeed. They will likely take the time to explain not only some of the terminology that may be difficult for you to grasp but also offer you other information that may help you to understand this child and how to set him or her up for success in your school.

Sharing Key Information with Teachers

In an inclusive program, an individualized learning plan (or a similar resource) should be created for each child with a special need. This written document is shared with teachers during orientation or before school begins. Though creating learning plans for each student may be too costly and time-consuming for many congregations, there are a variety of options for all program sizes and types.

A formal learning plan may be completed by the educator or a learning consultant. Typically, the learning consultant meets with the parents and reviews all written documentation provided before observing the child in the classroom. That information is then compiled into a learning plan. Each formal learning plan has two main sections: (1) a paragraph describing the student's diagnosis, including his or her strengths and weaknesses, and (2) a list of possible modifications the teacher can incorporate into the classroom to set the student up for success. Modifications should be specific to the layout of the classroom or learning space. These might include adaptations of teacher instruction and expectations, goals for the student, additional learning aides, and physical changes for the classroom. An example of a learning plan can be found in Appendix G (page 125).

In place of a learning plan, the educator may choose to copy the classroom accommodation page directly from the student's IEP or psycho-educational report and present that to the teachers. Information for the teacher(s) can also be communicated by e-mail or in an abbreviated version of a learning plan. Having a written document is especially effective in helping teachers process the information and can serve as a resource to which teachers can refer throughout the year.

Finding Help

As we mentioned earlier, most likely you'll find people in your community who will help you to implement an inclusion program enthusiastically and with a wide range of background knowledge and information. These people may serve as advisors to the educator or learning consultant, form as a committee empowered to make decisions regarding the nature of the program, or even act in place of a learning consultant if the congregation cannot afford a paid professional. The following is a list of those who might be available to help:

- Lay leaders
- Community leaders
- Special education teachers
- Therapists
- Experienced teachers
- Experienced parents

Though there are multiple ways to recruit these leaders for your program, simple word of mouth is often the best method. A congregation's database is the first place to start. While these professionals and leaders may not have children in your program, as members of a religious community, they will likely be willing to offer their consultation services to their congregational school for free or for a minimal fee. Though it may not be evident from a database, there may be parents and teachers who have personal experience with special needs and may be able to help. To reach these individuals, an article in your congregation's bulletin by you or your clergyperson may inspire them to step up. If there are no individuals in your congregation with these skills, Jewish Family Services, Jewish Federations, and other non-Jewish nonprofit counseling services may offer a wealth of resources, connections, or referrals to people who may provide low-cost services.

Some Simple Classroom and School Accommodations

Creating an inclusive school is a slow and thoughtful process. It should be implemented at a pace that is comfortable for teachers, clergy, and staff. Some of the changes will be challenging and others will feel like natural educational modifications. It is best to begin with the low-hanging fruit that make a big impact with little expense. Many of these modifications may seem obvious to teachers or educators; nonetheless, they should be reemphasized regularly.

Educators, in partnership with a learning consultant, should regularly examine the layout of classrooms. Without micromanaging, it is the duty of the educator to share feedback with teachers about proper classroom setup. Essentially, the room should be arranged in a way that gives all students easy visual access to the board and to the teacher. Frequently, teachers set up pods or groupings of tables around the room. This is fine as long as the teacher has a plan for students to face him or her when speaking and to see the board. However, within a religious school setting, where Hebrew is being taught, a better setup is a U, with the teacher and the board at the opening, or rows or semicircles facing the teacher and the board. In self-paced programs, such as the URJ's *Mitkadem* Hebrew program, this classroom model should be utilized in smaller formations, such as allowing students to sit on three sides of a small table, with an opening for the teacher, or in smaller U-shaped pods of desks. In all designs, preferential or strategic seating of students with special needs should always be considered. The goal of seating strategies is to meet the student's individualized needs (whether they're visual, auditory, behavioral, etc.). For students with sensory and movement needs, it may be optimal to seat them toward the back or on the periphery so that their movements cause minimal distraction to their classmates. Students with attention and processing difficulties typically benefit from placement close to the teacher or close to an assistant. In all classroom formations, be sure not to create a situation in which a child feels isolated or ostracized by being seated alone or outside the group. This can be prevented by placing a *tzadik(ah)* next to the student to provide extra one-on-one assistance.

Once classrooms are set up properly to allow for visual access to the teacher and the board, thought should be given to placement of all students. For teachers who like to move students around regularly, name cards can be made for all students. When the teacher places the cards on the desks at the beginning of the day, he or she has the flexibility to strategically place students with special needs.

It is also important for teachers to design their classrooms with special needs in mind. To accomplish this, they should limit distractions around the board, such as additional charts and pictures taped on the surface; set up proper student workstations that have ample room for books and papers for both right-handed and left-handed children; and be sure that any learning tools, such as *Alef-Bet* charts or assignment instructions, are clearly visible to all students. Other suggestions include setting up additional learning stations in quiet corners for one-on-one attention; making sure that dry erase markers or chalk are new and write clearly on the board; posting clear and succinct classroom rules, worded in a positive way (see Appendix E, page 121, that are visible to all students; and writing on the board each day an outline of daily activities.

Teachers can also make texts and textbooks more accessible to all students with little expense involved. When teaching Hebrew texts that will be used regularly, make an enlarged photocopy for each student, not just those with special needs. In *b'nei mitzvah* study binders, give every student a photocopied prayer packet with text and Torah portion and Haftarah portion that have been enlarged a minimum of 30 percent, in addition to the regular prayer packets and readings. You will probably find that most students (with or without special needs) choose to work from the enlarged text packets first and then eventually transition to the regular-sized copies. Additionally, the teacher can make transparencies to be projected onto the wall or scan the texts to be projected by LCD projectors or on SMART Boards. Highlighting a Hebrew text is an easy way to assist students with phonological awareness issues. This technique also helps many adults learn to read basic Hebrew by training them to break apart syllables before attempting to decipher full words. See page 62 for more details.

The *tzadikim* guide also provides strategies for teaching students with special needs. All fourteen of the strategies do not require special training and can be implemented immediately. Though many of them seem basic, such as using gestures or providing simple directions, these recommendations should be repeated regularly to all teachers to help them keep their own teaching styles fresh.

Chapter 4

The *Tzadikim* Program

As Moses led the Israelites across the Red Sea to freedom during the Exodus from Egypt, the people found it necessary to come to Moses to solve all their problems and address all their needs. In Exodus 18, Moses is taught a valuable lesson by his father-in-law Jethro about leadership and sharing responsibility: "Moses's father-in-law said to him, 'This thing you are doing is not good; you will surely wear yourself out, and your people as well. For the task is too heavy for you and you cannot do it alone'" (17–18). Jethro tells Moses to seek out from among the people capable men to appoint over the people to share the burden of his responsibility, thus forming an early model of shared leadership.

Creating an inclusive program would be an impossible task for an educator to do alone. Even with buy-in from the clergy and staff, the reality is that the educational team is going to do the majority of the work. But between phone calls and e-mails from teachers and parents, staff meetings, ongoing curriculum planning and programming, you may barely have enough time to improve or keep your existing programs running smoothly. Additionally, with so much time often spent on discipline issues and "putting out fires," you may wonder how you will be able to find the time to communicate a plan for inclusion to your teachers, let alone implement it.

Just as Moses had Aaron by his side, a learning consultant will be your partner in overseeing the program. However, the true leaders will come from the ranks of the capable assistants, or *tzadikim*, in your program. Teens have a distinctive way of connecting with and making learning fun for students with special needs. Teens are typically less intimidating than adults and when they pull younger students out of the classroom for one-on-one reinforcement, other children in the class often look at their peers with jealousy. With learning plans and *tzadikim* in place, you should find less of a need for regular communications with teachers about discipline issues, freeing up more time in your schedule. Thus the inclusion model and the teen volunteer program can provide benefits to the educator, in addition to creating a transformative experience for the teens themselves.

Creating Meaning for Teens

Middle school and high school students are busy. They are overworked in school, over-programmed in extracurricular activities, and bombarded by the message that "more is better" when it comes to getting into college. Most high school students are also required to complete a certain number of volunteer/community service hours for their school or to qualify for state-funded university scholarships. In the midst of all their requirements and extracurricular activities, teens are seeking personal and spiritual meaning in their own lives.

If you scan the Internet, you will find hundreds of outlets for teen "service learning." *Service learning* is the new buzzword in education for learning that combines community service with classroom instruction, allowing students to first learn through problem solving in real life situations, followed by reflection in the classroom. Many members of this generation of Jewish adolescents find Jewish connection through their community service work. Many congregations have drawn better attendance at and more positive feedback from social action trips and after-school projects than at social youth group events.

The *tzadikim* program can be an avenue for teens to find meaning in their Jewish spirituality. The program combines classroom guidance and learning with problem solving and one-on-one mentoring. As teen volunteers develop relationships with the students they serve, they become witness to their students' newfound sense of accomplishment in learning to read Hebrew, creating a Jewish art project, or even sitting in the chapel for all or the majority of *tefilah*, or prayer service. Educational leaders and clergy can add a sense of *kavod*, or respect, to the teens' work through regular words of praise, letters of gratitude, and public recognition at services or school programs.

Who Is a *Tzadik* or *Tzadikah*?

The *tzadikim* guide shows teenagers that their role as *tzadikim* means more than just being assistants in a classroom. The term *tzadikim* is used to connect a special needs assistant's work with the value of *tzedek*, or justice. Like Moses's instructions to the Israelites in Deuteronomy 16:2, "Justice, justice you shall pursue," students are introduced to the idea that their actions can affect the balance of justice in the world.

The role of a *tzadik* or *tzadikah* is a specific one. Though there are two potential assignments (to work one-on-one with a specific student or to work with multiple students in the learning lab), all *tzadikim* are trained with the same philosophy and with the same methodologies. All *tzadikim* are taught to learn the MUSIC of becoming effective *tzadikim*:

M odeling skills and behavior
U nderstanding your student's needs
S tudent advocacy
I mplementing behavioral management
C ommunicating with parents

Recruiting the First Cohort

Though Moses was introduced to the concept of sharing responsibility by his father-in-law, during the Israelites' wanderings he finds his own recruitment style. He tells the Israelites to pick from among them the wise and experienced and urges them "not [to] be partial in judgment; hear out low and high alike" (Deuteronomy 1:7). Recruiting *tzadikim* is a similar task, as the range of volunteers will have varied skills, characteristics, personalities, and experience.

Typically, the most successful *tzadikim* have previously worked as classroom *madrichim*. Though this is not critical, experience in classroom management allows the *tzadik* or *tzadikah* to dive right into implementing the *tzadikim* program's new strategies and learning techniques, rather than getting bogged down by first having to learn how to manage students in a classroom setting.

All kinds of students can do a great job as *tzadikim*. Assertive teens typically have an innate ability to manage the role, yet some of the more reserved and thoughtful students can make wonderful *tzadikim* as well. As a rule, boys often feel most comfortable with male *tzadikim* and girls more comfortable with *tzadikot*. But when dealing with children with complex physical needs (such as those with multiple needs, including gait imbalance when walking, intellectual disabilities, and drooling, etc.), girl-boy pairings may be considered and have proven highly successful in many cases. However, the educator should always keep in mind sexuality issues (i.e., if the child's diagnosis involves any sexually inappropriate behaviors) and physical size issues (i.e., pairing a stronger teen with a large child who is in a wheelchair) when pairing teens with children.

Recruitment can be conducted in two different ways: through a personal ask by a clergyperson or educator or through an application process. When first creating a program or in small congregations, the personal ask seems to work best. However, once the program is established and known in the community, an application process becomes more appropriate. Prerequisites should be determined before recruiting. Some suggested prerequisites are:

1. previous experience working as classroom *madrichim* or as camp counselors
2. a firm foundation in basic Hebrew
3. proven leadership skills (whether observed or through a specific program)
4. regular program attendance.

Though it may seem that *tzadikim* should not have specific special needs themselves, students who graduate from the program are often the most successful leaders. The most effective *tzadik* could be a student with dyslexia who has learned the Hebrew reading strategies himself while studying to become bar mitzvah.

Recruitment should begin well before students are eligible for the program. The *tzadikim* program should be publicized in the school handbook and in any listings of bar and bat mitzvah projects and high school social action projects. Clergy should also be reminded to speak about the program during meetings with students and families before and after *b'nei mitzvah*. End-of-year programs and services that honor *tzadikim* are also an effective tool for recruiting next year's *tzadikim*.

Even if recruitment is conducted by an application process, in the end the educators or clergy should be prepared to make personal asks to fill in any holes. Though it may seem as if this is circumventing the process, the ultimate goal is to provide the best assistance to the educational team and to the students.

When recruiting and selecting the first cohort of *tzadikim*, the goal should be to select and train more teenagers than needed to work as one-on-one assistants. This will keep a number of *tzadikim* available to work with students being pulled out of classrooms for reinforcement, as well as ready to go if the need arises for an additional shadow. Educators and learning consultants should also consider training students to work solely as general classroom assistants in their first year in the *tzadikim* program, not only to enhance their classroom skills, but also to have potential *tzadikim* waiting in the wings if you encounter a need for additional *tzadikim*. Though these students will begin the year as general classroom assistants, they can be given additional classroom responsibilities, such as one-on-one remedial Hebrew tutoring, giving additional assistance to a student with a minor special need (who does not require a full-time *tzadik*), or substituting for *tzadikim* when they are absent.

Interviewing and Accepting *Tzadikim*

Depending on the educator's relationship with the students and knowledge of their qualifications, the decision should be made whether to conduct formal interviews or to allow teenagers to apply through an application process. In either case, the goal of the process is to find empathetic and dedicated teenagers who are able to create a trusting relationship with students. Interview questions should focus on both these attributes, with questions eliciting personal experiences of working or interacting with individuals who are different.

Contracts should be provided to all *tzadikim*. The contract should clearly state the school's expectations, including time commitments for training sessions and weekly work schedules, expectations for communications with their students' parents and the learning lab coordinator, and what to do if they are sick or unable to attend a session. The contract may also be provided prior to acceptance as part of the application process, so that applicants are aware of the expectations for their work as *tzadikim* from the beginning.

Chapter 5

The *Tzadikim* Program: Training

Overview of *Tzadikim* Training Sessions

Once a core group of tzadikim has been selected, send acceptance letters or e-mails delineating a clear schedule for training and school dates. The most effective time for the orientation and first training session (Workshop I) is two to three weeks prior to the beginning of school. The first workshop takes three and a half to four hours[1] with the primary goals of establishing the role of *tzadikim*, helping them understand specific special needs, and presenting a variety of classroom and individualized teaching strategies for students who learn differently. Though Workshop I is broken down into three parts, it is recommended that you complete all three parts in one session and include lunch or dinner between parts. If a three-and-a-half-hour block of time is not available, then the session may be broken up into two two-hour sessions, no more than one week apart. (The first week would include mixers, Workshop I: part 1, and administrative guidelines. The second week would include a review of Workshop I: part 1 and administrative details, and completion of Workshop I: parts 2 and 3.)

A secondary goal of the first workshop is to create camaraderie and cohesion among *tzadikim*, the educator, and the learning consultant. This session may also be opened up to Hebrew or Judaic teachers; however, it should be made clear to them from the outset that the learning is geared for the teenage volunteers. Though the workshop includes several hands-on activities and empathy challenges, the facilitator should begin with a couple of icebreakers or mixers.

The other three workshops are about an hour in length each, and additional time should be provided for *tzadikim* to discuss their personal classroom issues with the learning consultant. These workshops are scheduled at key times throughout the year to give students a formal setting in which to discuss their work and receive feedback from their peers and their su-

1 This workshop can be shortened to three hours, but the additional half-hour allows for proper absorption of the materials and time for questions and answers.

pervisor. At the end of each session, the learning consultant should remind *tzadikim* to ask for direct assistance whenever needed.

Workshop II is intended to take place at the end of the first month of school (or after the third or fourth week working with students), once a relationship has developed between the *tzadikim* and their students. Case studies in this lesson guide participants through situations in which they must be proactive with teachers to help their students succeed and help them understand the difference between special needs and those who simply act out in class. This session also reminds *tzadikim* to be mindful of other students' learning in the classroom and how to best advocate for them.

The next workshop (III) is intended to serve as a midyear reflection. It enables *tzadikim* to take a step back and evaluate their students' progress and pitfalls and focuses on when the *tzadikim* should seek professional guidance. Role-playing scenarios also assist *tzadikim* in problem-solving techniques.

The final workshop, to be conducted during the last few weeks of school, is designed to help both the school and the *tzadikim*. Evaluation of students with special needs by *tzadikim* assists the learning consultant in updating learning plans for the following year. In addition, this workshop helps *tzadikim* evaluate their own progress as special needs facilitators and as leaders.

Selecting a Learning Venue

Choosing the right venue for *tzadikim* meetings and training sessions is one of the most important aspects of the program. Just as you select a particular hairstyle or a wardrobe, the style of the meetings send a message about the program to the teen community. The planning team (the educator and the learning consultant) should carefully balance what would be most attractive to teens for recruitment purposes with what would be most effective for facilitating learning and open discussions.

Due to its length, the first workshop should take place in a comfortable environment. Though much of the workshop requires desktop activities, it is recommended not to hold it in a classroom. Instead, a large meeting or conference room with round tables and space for kinesthetic mixers and activities will create a professional but relaxed atmosphere. A large family room or finished basement also offers an open and comfortable environment. Follow-up meetings may be held in a smaller setting, but thought should be given to the atmosphere created by that location as well.

Though there is a formal written curriculum, it is designed to be hands-on, with open discussion between the presenter and the learners. Because *tzadikim* are hand-selected, the facilitator should verbally and nonverbally show an immediate sense of trust in the participants while teaching. This includes allowing *tzadikim* to read out loud (rather than lecturing or reading to them), asking for direct feedback and personal examples, and showing great interest in their opinions (on this subject and others). In setting the times for meetings and workshops, the leaders should build in extra time (approximately 15 to 20 minutes) for questions and other tangents to the discussion. Remember, *tzadikim* are the on the front line of the program, so it is important for them to feel heard and recognized for their critical role in the daily workings of the program.

As with any successful Jewish program, food (budgeted into program costs or provided by lay leaders) is essential to the success of meetings and workshops. Since the program is based on *tzadikim* building relationships with their students, meetings around a table or tables with food offer a "family dinner table" atmosphere, conducive to sharing personal experiences and forging relationships. Whether it is dessert, snacks, or a full meal, participants will also feel privileged to be eating at the same table as their teachers.

Workshop Facilitator's Guide

Workshop I: Facilitating the Curriculum

In the welcome letter or meeting notification before each meeting, include the "Self-Study Exercises" found at the beginning of each workshop session in the *tzadikim* guide. Prior to the meeting, the facilitator should decide when to go over or discuss the participants' answers. Asking participants one or more of the questions at the beginning of each workshop may serve as a good discussion starter, or the facilitator may choose to ask the questions during the meal to facilitate conversation then.

As noted earlier, the first workshop should begin with one or more icebreakers or mixers to build trust and open dialogue among participants. When selecting icebreakers or mixers, be sure that they include elements of getting to know each other's names and personalities. A nice mix of kinesthetic and mental activities will energize participants for learning. Examples for groups of at least ten participants include Question Ball (a beach ball or a soft plastic ball with 20 fun questions written all over it in permanent marker is thrown back and forth between participants and each must answer the question that is closest to his or her face) and human BINGO (where each participant receives a grid of boxes with different facts about the people in the room and participants must walk around to find someone who matches each description). Smaller groups may enjoy Two Truths and a Lie (each participant presents two true facts and one made-up fact about him- or herself and the other participants try to guess which is not true) or Commercials (participants are divided into pairs and are asked to interview each other to present their partner to the group in commercial form). Prepare an additional short mixer for later in the session, in case participants need a break from the more intense elements of the workshop.

Required and recommended materials for Workshop I:

- A variety of writing instruments (pens, pencils, markers)
- Copies of the ***tzadikim*** contract (to review ***tzadikim*** responsibilities)
- A schedule of workshop meeting times and religious or Hebrew school class dates
- Mirrors (one for each pair of participants,[2] dollar stores typically sell 8 x 10 frame mirrors)
- A whiteboard or flip chart
- Examples of reward and incentive charts[1] (individual pads or posters; these can be purchased at a teacher supply store, office supply store, or dollar store)
- Reward stickers, like stars, smiley faces, "good work," etc. (enough for each of the participants to take with them)
- Bendable colored wax sticks, moldable dough, and/or pipe cleaners
- Small Torah pointers, chopsticks, eraser tips, or other tools for pointing while reading
- Highlighters (at least enough for each participant to receive two colors; avoid using red and green together because of color confusion among children with red-green color-blindness.)
- An enlarged Hebrew sentence or passage from a prayer (a sentence from a prayer enlarged on a copier; participants will use this to practice color-coding syllable division with highlighters, as described in the training manual)
- Information about the students each ***tzadik*** will be assisting (preferably in the form of a learning plan), including parent contact information

---

2 While there are new movements trending away from the use of extrinsic rewards, charts and stickers can be effective for many children.

The workshop is best presented seminar-style, with the instructor (or instructors) and the group seated around a large round table or long tables set in a square. The instructor introduces each section briefly and then has participants volunteer to read. As participants are reading, the instructor should model some of the techniques taught in the session, such as writing the page number on the board and writing some of the highlighted words or concepts on the board (such as forms of the word *tzadik*, MUSIC and the meanings of the letters in this acronym, etc.) and then pointing to them as they are discussed. Only call on those who volunteer to read. Additionally, the instructors should highlight certain concepts with comments or examples of their own and encourage contributions from participants. Group work, in pairs or groups of three, is encouraged during activities and exercises.

The curriculum is designed with empathy challenges and hands-on participation as key elements. As the workshop leader, you need to work through the challenges and activities first on your own, so that as participants are working through them, you will also be empathetic to their frustrations or questions. The following sections will guide the facilitator through the challenges and provide space for you to take your own notes.

WORKSHOP I

Although it is not necessary to review all the self-study answers with participants, this guide provides follow-up and trigger questions for all the self-study questions. You may wish to use a highlighter to mark the questions or exercises you will cover in this session. You should not spend more than ten minutes on the self-study review.

Participants are often nervous about sharing their own answers at first. Prepare your own example to share if there is a long silence in the group. Remember that short silences (5- to 10-second pauses after the question or between answers) are natural and important. Be careful not to jump in too quickly to offer your own answer.

As participants share their new skills, ask: "How did you feel when you first started to [perform the skill just named]?" Note that the goal of most of the exercises in these workshops is to get participants in touch with their own feelings. When asking for participants to talk about their feelings, be sure to only accept answers that are really feelings. Scared, timid, uneasy, and excited all describe feelings, but answers such as fine, the same, and like everyone else do not reflect feelings.

Self-Study Exercises

(to be completed prior to attending Workshop I)

Think of a situation when you were learning a new skill and write it below. An example of this may be learning to swim, ride a bike, or skate. What were some of the basic skills you needed to know in order to succeed? Examples for swimming are "holding your breath," "kicking," etc.

New skill: ______________________

____

____

____

____

____

____

Basic skills needed to succeed at this: ______________________

____

____

____

____

____

____

____

____

____

____

____

____

Refer to Workbook page 140

As you probably remember, learning a new skill takes patience, practice, and concentration. In acquiring most new skills, we succeed within a relatively short time. As with all new endeavors, we begin by building on skills we have previously learned. For example, before we learned to read, we learned the letters and their sounds, and before we learned how to play baseball, we learned how to run, throw and catch a ball, swing a bat, and so on. But, if we do not have the basic skills (such as knowledge of the letters or how to throw a ball), learning more complex skills is nearly impossible.

Not all children learn basic skills at the same pace and many children are born without the ability to learn basic skills easily. For most of us, crawling and walking came naturally within our first eighteen months. Yet there are many babies and toddlers who must work with physical and occupational therapists to teach them these basic skills.

Think back to your childhood. Are there any basic skills that were difficult for you to learn? What are some skills that are still challenging for you?

Basic skills that were hard for you to learn: ______________________

____

____

____

____

____

____

____

As participants share the more difficult skills, ask: "How did you [or do you] feel when you had [or have] trouble [performing the skill just named]?

Skills that are still challenging for you: ______________________

____

____

____

____

____

____

____

____

____

Note: If participants are having trouble naming feelings, take a break from the text questions and work on naming feelings. You may want to start with a simple exercise brainstorming feelings.
Ask the group to name as many feelings or emotions as they can and have a participant record them on a whiteboard or flip chart. Examples include happy, sad, uncomfortable, emotional, scared, excited, reticent, angry, embarrassed,
elated, worried, joyful, crazy, silly, and so on.
Next, present a situation and ask the group toshare some possible feelings or emotions. For example, "Before a very difficult test, I feel . . ." or "When I am getting ready to open a Chanukah present, I feel . . ." Suggest that participants consult the list of feelings that they brainstormed or challenge themselves to come up with additional ones.

Note: Allow participants to ask questions without your feeling obligated to give answers. Participants have prepared questions about disabilities or learning differences they have seen in the past. As they present their own answers, acknowledge them with a positive comment (such as "Good one" or "Interesting") or a nod, but do not answer their questions. If you feel that there is a question that needs to be answered, you may choose to keep a list under the heading "Parking Lot" on a whiteboard or flip chart to be answered later in the session or during a break.

The students you will be working with over the next year are not typical learners. Though outsiders may or may not easily recognize their differences, each of these students learns or develops at a different pace than their peers. Some of these students don't even recognize that they are different from their peers. Your role is to assist these students by utilizing strategies that are designed to remove many of the barriers that hinder their learning and allow them to participate in Jewish learning alongside their peers. During the upcoming workshop, you will learn about some common learning differences that you may encounter.

Throughout your life, you have probably seen or met individuals with disabilities or learning differences. Think of a specific person you have encountered in the past (in person or on television or in the movies).

1. When you saw him or her, how did you feel? Carefully describe your emotions. ______________________________

____

____

____

____

____

2. Do you know what type of disability or learning difference he or she has? If so, what is it? ______________________________

____

____

____

____

____

3. What questions do you have about his or her differences? ______________________________

____

____

____

____

____

In religious school, you studied the holidays, history, and traditions of Judaism. If you became a bar or bat mitzvah, you probably began studying commentaries on the Torah and other Jewish texts. Our great Sages have been commenting on and discussing our heritage and traditions for thousands of years.

As with most topics, Judaism has a lot to say about those who learn differently. During the first workshop, you will explore what our tradition says about this. Before we study it as a group, think about some of the precepts and stories you learned about Judaism.

What do you think that Jewish tradition says about how we should treat those who are different? Describe at least one idea or story from our tradition that deals with differences. Feel free to list any quotes from the Bible or commentators, if you remember them.

Examples:

"And Moses said to God, 'I am not a man of words. . .'" (Exodus 4:10)

The commentator Rashi explains that Moses had a stammer or a stutter.

"You shall not . . . place a stumbling block before the blind . . ." (Leviticus 19:14).

This is a commandment to take care of the blind, but in this context blind can also be understood as referring to any disability or difference.

Leprosy, or infections with white scales, is mentioned frequently in the Book of Leviticus.

The Torah also talks about specific laws for those with this disease or diseases of impurity.

Notes: Many participants may not feel confident when it comes to biblical references, so consider adopting the following strategies:

- You may need to prompt participants to answer biblical questions by hinting at specific stories. For instance, you may ask participants to think of any diseases or impurities mentioned in the Torah to prompt a discussion of leprosy. Alternatively, you may ask participants to give a brief summary of their bar or bat mitzvah Torah portions and then look for examples of unfair treatment of others in their specific Torah portions.
- Be sure to acknowledge that Torah study is quite difficult, especially when we are trying to think of specific examples. All answers, whether correct or not, should be positively acknowledged. This is a way to model positive feedback for participants who will be working with children who learn differently.

Notes: Provide positive acknowledgment for all answers, along the following lines:

- Remember to redirect any negative or derogatory examples.
- If participants' descriptions of how learning differences affect children are inaccurate, it is not necessary to correct them unless they are completely wrong. For instance, if a participant says ADHD causes a child to misbehave, there's no need to give any additional information. However, if he or she says that ADHD causes the child to yell out profanities, you may choose to say, "I don't think that is a characteristic of ADHD, but we will be learning about ADHD and its characteristics later today in our lesson."

In the Passover seder, we are reminded about how to treat others, because we were once strangers in the Land of Egypt. The goal of the seder is to reenact the experience of our ancestors' slavery in Egypt. Similarly, the key to becoming a successful mentor to a student with special needs is understanding learning differences and how they affect students. Your knowledge of these differences will assist you in becoming an empathetic leader.

Are there any learning differences with which you are already familiar? Name one or more and attempt to describe how they affect children.

Learning difference: ______________________________

____

____

____

____

How it affects the child: ______________________________

____

____

____

____

Learning difference: ______________________________

____

____

____

____

How it affects the child: ______________________________

____

____

____

____

Refer to Workbook page 145

Prepare:

• Before teaching this section, it is important for the educator, the learning consultant, and/or the instructor to become fluent in the use of the word *tzadikim* and its conjugated forms.

• The instructor (or educator or learning consultant) should write the word MUSIC (in all capital letters) on the whiteboard or flipchart with the acrostic below:

M odeling skills and behavior
U nderstanding your student's needs
S tudent advocacy
I mplementing behavior management
C ommunicating with parents

• For the empathy challenge, one mirror is needed for every two participants.

For the following sections, the facilitator should encourage participants to volunteer to read each section out loud. However, in the interest of time, the facilitator may choose to read some of the longer and more complex sections him- or herself. Ask (after reading):

• What do you think is the difference between a *madrich* and a *tzadik*?

• The facilitator should make sure that participants understand that *tzadikim* are responsible for working one-on-one with specific students and to help students with differences fo be successful in the classroom.

WORKSHOP I

Part 1: What Is a *Tzadik(ah)*?

Objectives: By the end of this workshop, you will be able to:

- Understand the meaning of the words *tzadik, tzadikah, tzadikim,* and *tzadikot* and use these words correctly.
- Outline the roles of *tzadikim*.
- Understand what *tzadikim* do in the classroom.
- Describe the centrality of helping others in Jewish tradition.

Who Are *Tzadikim*?

In the Israelites' quest to become a holy people, deserving of entering the Promised Land, Moses instructs them, "Justice, justice shall you pursue" (Deuteronomy 16:2). In Hebrew, the word for "justice" is *tzedek*, and those who work to bring a greater measure of justice to the world are called *tzadikim*. Throughout our tradition, Jews have striven to act righteously. The Talmud teaches that in every generation there are thirty-six righteous people (called *lamed-vavniks*, from the Hebrew letters *lamed* and *vav* that represent the number thirty-six) who are ordinary, humble, and hidden among us. God allows the world to continue to exist because these *lamed-vav tzadikim* are living in our community and sustaining us without our even knowing it.

Today, you begin your journey as a *tzadik* or *tzadikah*. Like *tzadikim* in the generations before us, you too have a unique challenge to pursue justice in the world. As a religious school *tzadik* or *tzadikah*, you will bring justice to our world by helping a child who was born with a special need succeed in Jewish learning. As a trained teaching assistant working individually with students with special needs, you will make sure your students are not stigmatized or separated from their peers. Though your students need one-on-one assistance in their learning, it is our goal to make sure that they do not feel any different than the rest of the students in their class. Though you may have additional *madrichim*, or assistants, working in your school, your team's specialized skills will blend in with the rest of the school. Yet you will learn that without you and your specialized teaching methods, classroom learning cannot succeed. Like the *lamed-vav tzadikim*, you will help sustain the overall success of the class. Thus with the righteous work you are about to embark on, you are taking on the name and the goal of *tzadikim*.

But before you begin, it is important to learn to use the Hebrew word for "righteous one" correctly. A male is called a *tzadik* (צַדִּיק) and a female is called a *tzadikah* (צַדִּיקָה). The plural of *tzadik* is *tzadikim* (צַדִּיקִים) and the feminine plural is *tzadikot* (צַדִּיקוֹת).

Rachel and Lily are called tzadikot .

Michael is a tzadik .

Robert and Jill are tzadikim .

Beth is a tzadikah .

The Role of *Tzadikim*

Though every day may be different working with your student, you are charged with certain responsibilities that will help your student succeed. Just as you move to a certain rhythm in the way you interact in the world, you must also learn the **MUSIC** of becoming an effective *tzadik* or *tzadikah:*

M odeling skills and behavior
U nderstanding your student's needs
S tudent advocacy
I mplementing behavioral management
C ommunicating with parents

The most effective *tzadikim* model techniques for learning, understand their student's needs, advocate for their student in the classroom, assist with behavior management, and maintain constant communication with their student's parents. Through the next few exercises, you will begin to learn the MUSIC of being a righteous one.

Modeling

If you have been a *madrich* or *madrichah* (a classroom assistant) in your religious school, you know the importance of being a role model for your students. *Madrichim* learn that modeling respectful behavior and other positive actions teach students how to act in the classroom. As a *tzadik* or *tzadikah,* you should always model techniques that will assist students in successful learning. For example, when you read Hebrew, you should use your finger to follow along. This helps you focus on the individual word or syllable that you are reading. Though you may read Hebrew well without using your finger, modeling this strategy will make the action seem more natural for your student. In addition, other students in the class may pick up on your behavior and also begin to use this strategy.

If you are assigned to work with a boy who has hearing problems (even with a hearing aid), what are some simple behaviors that you could model to help him succeed in class? (Think about his seating location, what he should do when others are speaking, etc.)

Be sure to point out the acronym MUSIC, writtenon the board or flip chart. By presenting the concept in a larger format than that of the printed workbook, you are modeling a learning technique for working with students with special needs. This and other techniques that will be taught in the workshops are also helpful for traditional learners.

Possible Answers:

- Sit close to the teacher or instructor.
- Speak slowly and clearly.
- Face the child when speaking to him or her (so he or she can read your lips).

Understanding

All children are different and have different learning and physical needs. In this workshop, almost everyone is processing the lesson differently. Some people in the room learn better by hearing the information verbally and others must read it or see it to understand it. A few people in the room may have "photographic memories" and can memorize all the details on the page, while others may be color-blind, thus affecting the way colored texts and pictures look to them. If you have ever recorded your voice on a phone or a digital recorder, you will notice that it sounds different to you when you play it back. This is a simple way of understanding how others may hear things differently.

- ***Empathy Challenge***

Your facilitator is going to give you a mirror and a pencil. Have a partner place the mirror just to the left of the star on the line so that the star will reflect into the mirror. Looking only at the star in the mirror, trace the star with your pencil.

As participants are paired up and begin the empathy challenge of tracing the star while looking in the mirror, walk around the room to guide the partner tracing the star to focus on the mirror and not to look at the page. Participants will get frustrated and even become embarrassed. You may want to share some encouraging comments with those who are not succeeding (such as, "Remember not to go outside the lines" or "Nice job . . . you can do it").

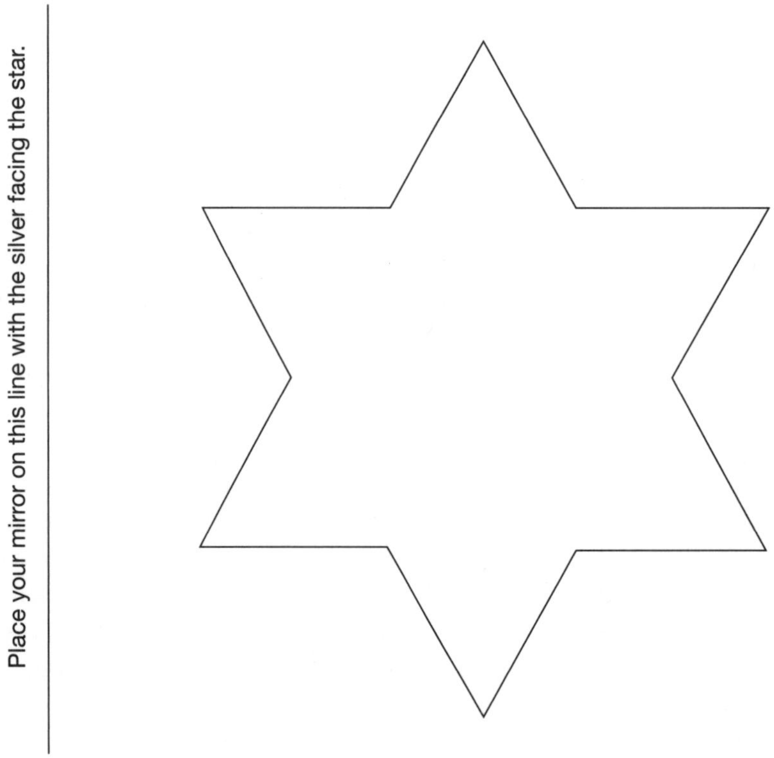

Place your mirror on this line with the silver facing the star.

When you have finished tracing the star, have your partner complete the same exercise.

(Answer the following question after both of you have completed the exercise)

How well did you do? Describe how you felt as you were trying to trace the star. ______________________________

____

____

____

After participants have completed the exercise, ask:

- How did you feel when you were attempting to trace the star? (Remember to elicit emotions or feelings.)
- What do you think was the point of this exercise? (Possible answers: to help us understand what it feels like to be different or to struggle, to empathize with students with special needs, etc.)
- How do you think you would react during exercises like this if you always struggled with classwork?

This exercise was a simple example to show you how it feels to learn differently. When it was over, you were able to remove the mirror and go back to "normal." Think about what it would feel like if your perception and vision were always like this. What would it be like playing baseball, eating candy out of a small bag, or reading a book?

When you spend time with your student over the next year, try to imagine what it would be like to live with his or her needs every day. You may wish to use the pages in the back of this book to write down thoughts and feelings as your experience them.

Student Advocacy

Living with a learning difference not only makes everyday tasks and learning challenging, it also makes interacting in the world more difficult. Many special needs are not seen by the outside world. For example, when a child has difficulty hearing, people often think he or she is rude because he or she does not respond when someone says "hello."

As a *tzadik* or *tzadikah*, it is your responsibility to advocate, or stand up, for your student. For example, when a teacher plays a game, randomly calling on students to read from their books, a student with learning needs may not process the request at the same speed as the other students. Oftentimes, this will cause embarrassment as the other children in the class giggle, make condescending comments, or pressure him or her to answer.

Ask: (Before beginning the section on student advocacy, the facilitator may wish to introduce the concept of advocacy with the following questions.)

- What do you think it means to advocate for something?
- When have you seen or heard of people advocating for something? (Possible answers: protesting for increases in the minimum wage, civil rights marches, gay pride parades, etc.)

If your teacher plays a game like this regularly in class, and you notice this happening to your student, what would you do to advocate for him or her?

____

____

____

____

____

Notes:

- The answer to the question in this section is a difficult one and one that may require some group discussion. You may wish to prompt participants by asking a question like this: "Who could you speak to in order to advocate for the child you're shadowing and what would you say?" (Possible answers: the teacher, explaining that the game is causing your student to be embarrassed; the learning coordinator or a rabbi, asking for advice on how to alleviate the student's anxiety; etc.)
- Advocacy can take many different forms, so be sure to positively acknowledge all answers.

Implementing Behavior Management

Oftentimes, there is a correlation between special needs and negative behavior patterns. Some children with learning needs are active and cannot focus on the activity at hand. Other children cannot keep up with the "regular" pace of the class and therefore are constantly reprimanded for not following directions. Still other students' minds operate at such high levels that they get bored and move ahead to another thought before the teacher finishes explaining the lesson at hand. They subsequently get blamed for not paying attention.

Though these children disrupt the normal flow in the classroom, most of the time their negatively perceived behaviors are not their fault. As a *tzadik* or *tzadikah,* it is your role to assist your student in managing his or her behavior. This can be done in a variety of ways, but mostly it is accomplished by creating a behavior management system. Star charts, rewards, and regular reminders (nonverbal cues, such as a wink, a tap on the shoulder, etc.) are all systems that can be set up by *tzadikim*. The most important thing to remember is that behavior management should always be positive to promote positive behavior.

Notes:

- Prepare examples of positive reward systems of your own to share with participants. (Examples might include read-a-thons, getting a lollipop after seeing a doctor or dentist, etc.)
- Point out some systems that do not succeed, such as giving out so many rewards that they no longer feel special.

Think back to your own childhood. What kind of positive reward system(s) did your parents or your teachers create for you? Describe a system like this and how you felt when you succeeded. ______________

____

____

____

____

____

____

Prepare:

- By the end of the workshop, provide participants with the names of the parents of the students with whom they will be working, the parents' phone numbers and e-mail addresses, and any other important information (such as if the parents are divorced, if they are from another country, etc.).

Communicating with Parents

Your final role as a *tzadik* or *tzadikah* is to be the link between the school and the parents. Parents of students with special needs often need additional support and reinforcement from their children's teachers. Because the classroom teacher is responsible for communicating with all parents of students in the class, he or she often does not have the time to communicate sufficiently with the parents of those with special needs. As a *tzadik* or *tzadikah,* you are charged with the additional responsibility of supporting your child's parents.

If you are going to be absent, it is crucial for you to let your student's parents (and your program coordinator) know, so that alternate arrangements can be made. Also, when you notice that a particular strategy is successful with your student, you should let the child's parents know so that they can utilize that

Refer to Workbook page 150

strategy at home and share that strategy with the teacher(s) in the child's weekday school. Alternatively, if your strategies are not working, a parent can be a good source of assistance and support in finding another strategy that may work better for your student. Whatever the communication involves, it is important to remember that communication with parents should always be positive, even if the day was not a successful one for the student.

Give an example of a positive communication that you might share with parents about their child. (This can be a comment about the student's behavior, interactions with the teacher or other students, or about his or her class work.) ____________________

Follow-up Questions (after participants answer the question at the end of the section):

- "What are some positive words or phrases that you can use when speaking to parents?" (You may wish to list them on the board or flip chart and have participants copy them in to the notes section at the end of the workbook.)
- Possible answers: improved, patient, respectful, appropriate, friendly, shared, paid attention, played nicely, took his or her time, participated, helped, thanked, was polite, etc.
- Once a list of words or phrases is developed, you may wish to have participants practice using them in complete sentences.
For example, "Michael's participation improved today during our discussion on Purim," Rachel patiently waited her turn to write her answer on the whiteboard today."

Practice:

- Before participants answer the question on positive communications, the instructor should role-play scenarios with them. (These exercises may be done at the end of the session, instead of here, if you think that will work better with your group.) Some suggested scenarios are:
- Calling parents to introduce themselves and explaining that they will be a child's tzadik or tzadikah.
- Asking parents the best way to communicate with them (e.g., by phone or by e-mail).
- Meeting parents on the first day of school.
- Greeting the parents at the end of the day and telling them how well-behaved their child was in music today.
- Greeting the parents at the end of the day and sharing with them that it seemed as if their child was more frustrated in Hebrew than usual.
- During these role plays, provide specific and positive feedback.
- Remind participants that even though they are used to texting, they should be sure to find out the way the parents prefer to communicate. Explain to them that text messages can often be misinterpreted and, therefore, spoken conversations (by phone or in person) are the most effective method of communication

Judaism and Helping Others

About 3,700 years ago, when three visitors appeared at their tent, Abraham and Sarah modeled a behavior that would set a high standard for the future of Judaism. Rather than letting the strangers suffer in the heat of the desert, they invited them into their tent for water, cake, and rest. This is the origin of the Jewish value of welcoming the stranger.

Abraham's care for others was also shown when he argued with God in order save the people of Sodom and Gomorrah. Unlike those who came before him, he risked his life for others by challenging God on their behalf: "Will you sweep away the innocent along with the guilty? Shall not the Judge of all the earth deal justly?" (Genesis 18:23, 25) Through Abraham's model of care for others, our tradition has taught the importance of hospitality and looking out for the stranger.

Ever since the days of Abraham and Sarah, our texts and the leaders of our people have stood up for equality and fair treatment of others. The *Tanach* (the Hebrew Bible), our sacred writings, and our Sages have all shared insights on this subject.

Refer to Workbook page 151

Read over the Jewish texts on the left side of the page and try to match them to the interpretations on the right.

Answers: A6, B3, C1, D7, E8, F2, G5, H4

A You shall not . . . place a stumbling block before the blind. Leviticus 19:14	A synagogue should be a place where all people are welcomed. 1
B Look not at the container but at what it contains. Pirkei Avot 4:27	We should always make sure that others get the same respect that we do, no matter who they are. 2
C For My house shall be called a house of prayer for all peoples. Isaiah 56:7	Sometimes there is something special hidden inside a person that may not be easily seen from the outside. 3
D All your children shall be students of Adonai. Isaiah 54:13	You should treat everyone the same way that you hope to be treated. 4
E All of Israel is responsible for one another. Shavuot 39a	God will not look favorably in the future on those who make fun of or shame others. 5
F Let your friend's honor be as precious to you as your own. Pirkei Avot 2:10	If someone is at a disadvantage, we should be careful not to make his or her way any more difficult. 6
G One who... publicly shames a fellow human being..., that person would have no portion in the world to come. Pirkei Avot 3:11	All Jewish children shall be given the opportunity to study Judaism. 7
H Love your neighbor as yourself. Leviticus 19:18	As Jews, we should take care of all of our people. 8

WORKSHOP I

Part 2: Understanding Learning Differences and Learning Plans

Objectives: By the end of this workshop, you will be able to:

Prepare:

- Copies of student learning plans (or the accommodations section of IEPs or verbal information about the student to be shared) should be available for distribution to *tzadikim* at the end of this lesson.
- Highlighters should be available for participants to highlight important parts of their student's learning plan.

- Understand descriptions of key learning differences.
- Interpret the basic information in a learning plan.
- Describe your student's learning needs.

Understanding Different Types of Special Needs

Students with special needs may learn differently for a variety of reasons. Some may have difficulty with their fine-motor skills, which means they may have trouble cutting out a picture or writing with a regular pencil. Some students may have trouble listening to the teacher and following directions, not because they are misbehaving, but rather because they have difficulty understanding what is being said. Some students may not be able to pay attention for long periods of time, while other students may have no trouble listening but be unable to remember the specific sound associated with a Hebrew letter.

- ***Empathy Challenge***

After participants complete the empathy challenge, ask: "What does this exercise teach us about students with special needs?" (Possible answers: "Students with special needs often feel behind or confused," "It's very frustrating when we don't feel that we can catch up," "Students with learning differences should be given one short instruction at a time.")

Work with a partner. Read the following instructions to your partner and ask him or her to do exactly what you say. Speak at a normal speed, no faster or slower than you would normally speak:

"Find a blank page in either your book or in your backpack. Number the page from one to ten. Next to number three write down your favorite color, your favorite food next to number four, and next to number ten write down the person in Jewish history who means the most to you. Also, make sure that you write your first, last, and middle names and your age and grade on the top right-hand corner of the page. Next to number five, write the names of three Hebrew letters, and in the remaining blanks write five things you want for Chanukah. When you finish, turn your page over and raise your hand."

Refer to Workbook page 154

Discuss the following questions with your partner:

When you were trying to follow the directions, how did you feel and why?

How would you feel if you were listening to these directions in the classroom and you were the only student who appeared not to be able to follow along with your teacher?

Students who learn differently have usually had an evaluation by a doctor, a psychologist, or a therapist specializing in their particular area of weakness. After a full evaluation has been completed, the parents are typically given a copy of the professional's report. The report includes a diagnosis that helps the parents better understand their child's particular needs. In addition, the report usually includes recommendations for therapy programs to help the child, special school services needed, and specific strategies for the child's teacher. Some of these children may go to a special private school or they may attend a public school and go to special education classes for all or part of their day. Children in the public schools often have what is called an IEP, or an individualized education program. An IEP includes specific strategies that should be used in the classroom to help the teacher ensure that the child succeeds.

Below is a list of common special needs that you may encounter in the *tzadikim* program. The purpose of this information is to help you become familiar with some of the most common types of special needs that are seen in children today. The definitions and examples do not provide a full picture of these complex diagnoses and are not intended to be used to help you diagnose students yourself. They are only intended to provide you with examples of manifestations of learning needs that you may encounter in your work as a *tzadik* or *tzadikah*.

As you begin to introduce participants to some key learning differences/special needs, note the following:

- This section is designed to introduce participants to a variety of diagnoses. It is not intended to be a thorough study of specific special needs; rather, it is intended as a way for participants to understand terms they may see on their students' learning plans. There is no need to quiz participants on the terms.

Refer to Workbook page 155

Attention-Deficit/Hyperactivity Disorder (ADHD): Students diagnosed with ADHD exhibit some or all of the following symptoms: inattention, distractibility, impulsivity, and hyperactivity.

• Introduce this section of the workshop by saying, "We are about to read over a number of special needs terms and examples of each one. Do not worry about learning all of them. You will be able to use your workbook as a reference when you hear or read about these terms in the future. Please be sure to stop the class at any time if you do not understand a word or an example."

- Inattention and distractibility mean the student has trouble focusing.
  Example: While the teacher is talking, Josh is staring at the Sukkot decorations on the bulletin board and he is listening to the noise in the hallway as the kindergarten class is walking to the library.
- Impulsivity causes students to deviate from classroom rules.
  Example: Jacob frequently yells out questions without raising his hand.
- Hyperactivity leads a child to have difficulty sitting for prolonged periods of time.
  Example: Michael is squirming in his seat while the rest of the third graders are sitting quietly.

Auditory Processing Disorder (APD): Students diagnosed with APD have difficulty understanding what they hear, even when they are trying their best to listen. They are often misidentified as having behavioral problems.

- *Example*: The frustrated teacher repeats three times for Jacob to turn to page 52 and subsequently yells at him for not paying attention, but Jacob does not have the ability to follow oral commands.

Autism: Students diagnosed with autism have difficulty with social interactions and communication. Depending on the severity of the condition, students with autism may not speak or may have a very limited vocabulary. They tend to have a difficult time in novel surroundings, such as a Sunday school classroom. They also have a hard time looking people in the eye. A related, less severe diagnosis is called Asperger syndrome.

- *Example*: Micah, who has Asperger syndrome, attends the weekend overnight fourth-grade retreat, but he appears as if he is in his own world, while the rest of the students interact with one another and their teachers.

Developmental Delays: Students diagnosed with developmental delays have not reached benchmarks for development in one or several of these areas: intelligence, language/speech, physical development, social/emotional development, and self-help skills. Down syndrome and cerebral palsy are examples of two disorders associated with developmental delays.

1 Hyperactivity takes many different forms in different children. While having trouble sitting still is a common example, it can also be exhibited through other behaviors, such as restlessness, fidgeting, or the constant touching of objects and people.

- Students with intellectual delays have difficulty learning at the same rate as their peers.
  Example: You are trying to teach Shayna that the letter *bet* sounds like *B*. You have gone over it with her multiple times. Once you begin teaching her the next letter, *gimel*, Shayna has already forgotten the sounds a *bet* makes.
- Students with speech or language delays may have trouble saying certain sounds, making their speech hard to understand, or they may have difficulty expressing what they want to say because they have a limited vocabulary.
  Example: You are trying to teach the difference between *shin* and *sin* to Chelsea, who has a speech delay. When she pronounces the letters, they both sound like the letter *S*.
- Students with physical delays may have gross-motor delays, meaning they cannot walk well or they may be in a wheelchair. Students with fine-motor delays may have difficulty using their hands.
  Example: Jonathan cannot complete an art project because he cannot hold scissors properly.
- Students with social/emotional delays may be socially immature, compared to the other children in their class, and they will subsequently have difficulty making friends or even just initiating a conversation with a peer.
  Example: Lori, a sixth-grade student, always sits by herself during break, playing with her stuffed animals, while the other girls laugh and talk about boys and movies.
- Students with delays in the self-help area have difficulty taking care of themselves.
  Example: Ashley needs help pulling down her pants so she can go the bathroom.

Dyslexia: Dyslexia is a language-based learning disability that may interfere with a child's ability to learn written and oral language, including reading. Students with dyslexia often have a hard time decoding (sounding out words), writing legibly, spelling, and reading, especially if they are asked to read aloud. When they are reading, they may encounter visual-perception problems. These students often have a difficult time learning how to read Hebrew and English.

- *Example*: When Alex is reading Hebrew, he complains that the words look as though they are moving on the page.

Learning Disabilities (LDs): Students diagnosed with a learning disability have normal intelligence, but they may struggle in one or more of the following areas: oral expression, listening comprehension, written expression, basic reading skills, and/or math calculation and reasoning. Depending on the type of learning disability they have, children may display a variety of different symptoms in the classroom.

- *Example:* Maggie has difficulty formulating her thoughts and the wrong words keep coming out when she is telling the class what she did for the Passover holiday.

Sensory Integration (SI) Issues: Students diagnosed with SI issues have difficulty processing everyday sensations, such as noises or touch. They may also exhibit unusual behaviors, such as avoiding or seeking out touch, movement, sounds, and sights.

- *Example*: Evan becomes abnormally scared when he hears the high-pitched sound of the fire alarm during a fire drill.

Tourette Syndrome: Tourette syndrome is a neurological disorder that causes tics. These are unwanted twitches, movements, or sounds that people make. Though children may have tics without having Tourette syndrome, children are only diagnosed with this condition when they have two tics that affect body movement and one that is a sound (all observed over the course of at least one year). Although children with Tourette syndrome may seem disrespectful, their tics are involuntary and may include inappropriate language or curse words.

Applying What You Learned

> Mrs. Goldman is beginning her lesson. All of her first-grade students are sitting in their seats and enthusiastically listening as Mrs. Goldman tells the story of Jonah and the whale. All her students are sitting, that is, except for Mark. Mark is moving around his seat and his eyes are darting all over the room. He suddenly blurts out, "I saw a whale once when I went to SeaWorld with my Mommy and Daddy last year. It was really big!"

What symptoms did Mark exhibit? ______________________________

____

____

____

____

Refer to Workbook page 158

Although we should never attempt to label or diagnose a student, given the symptoms above, does Mark display behaviors similar to any of the special needs you just learned about? If so, which one(s)? ____________

____

____

____

____

> Ms. Kushner is having the students in her third-grade Sunday school class each take a turn reading from their textbooks about Shabbat traditions. Sarah asks to go to the bathroom when it is her turn to read. She looks as if she is about to cry. The teacher asks a teaching assistant to go with Sarah. When they get into the hallway, Sarah bursts into tears and says, "I can't read out loud in front of the entire class. Everyone will think that I am so stupid! The words look funny on the page. I hate Sunday school!"

What were Sarah's issues and how did they make her feel about coming to Sunday school? ____

____

____

____

____

Were any of the special needs described above unfamiliar to you? If so, which one(s)? ____

____

____

1. ____

____

2. ____

____

Refer to Workbook page 159

Note:

Because there are different types of programs, the workbook explains that *tzadikim* may receive a learning plan, the accommodations section of an IEP, or a verbal description of the student to be mentored. Even though the information will not be presented until the next workshop, explain here which type of information you are going to present about the students with special needs in your program.

Understanding the Student You Will Be Shadowing

Students with special needs often have a one-on-one facilitator in a classroom to help them participate in classroom activities. These facilitators are typically called "shadows." As a *tzadik* or *tzadikah*, you may be assigned to one student whom you will shadow in the classroom. Some *tzadikim* will be assigned more than one student, especially if there are two students with mild learning differences who are in the same class. Other *tzadikim* may be assistants to the supervisor of the program, and may work with multiple students outside of their regular Sunday school class in order to provide specialized one-on-one Hebrew tutoring. If you are a *tzadik* or *tzadikah* assigned to more than one student, you must understand the specific needs of each one of your students.

Ideally, your synagogue's program supervisor will provide you with a learning plan for your student. Learning plans have two parts. The first part describes what learning problems your assigned student are having. The second part provides specific classroom management strategies. The purpose of this workshop session is to ensure that you understand how to interpret the first part of a learning plan.

Please note that your synagogue's resources may not allow for a full learning plan as outlined in this book. Instead, you may be provided with a psychological report or an individualized education program (IEP) from the student's secular school. An IEP includes information about how your student learns and specific classroom management strategies, as well as information that will not be applicable to what you are doing in the classroom (specific special education services, therapies, and goals, for example). If your program supervisor does not have any written information for you, he or she may just give you information verbally.

Applying What You Learned

Notes:

- Explain to participants that you are about to begin an exercise looking at a hypothetical student's special needs, in preparation for each of them to receive their own student's learning plan later in the session.
- The student chosen in the learning plan (Lindsay) has multiple severe special needs so participants can easily identify many of her disabilities and needs. Tell participants that many of the students with whom they will be working may not have needs as severe as Lindsay's.

LEARNING PLAN FOR LINDSAY (PART 1)

Lindsay has a medical condition that causes developmental delays. such as walking, cutting, holding a pencil, speaking, and understanding classroom content. She has had no behavior problems over the last two years at Sunday school. She enjoys music and is able to attend the music activities without much supervision. Lindsay has delayed social skills and thus has difficulty initiating social contact with her peers. She has successfully participated in class with the assistance of a student from the *tzadikim* program for three years, and she enjoys the individualized attention. When Hebrew phonics were introduced at a more accelerated pace, her *tzadik* took her out of the classroom and worked one-on-one with Lindsay to help her learn and review Hebrew letters. It is not expected that Lindsay will be able to learn all the skills being taught this year, and she will be having an adapted bat mitzvah ceremony. So the teacher should not worry if Lindsay is learning the same amount of Hebrew as the other students. The goal is for Lindsay to continue to have a positive experience on Sundays.

Refer to Workbook page 160

After reading the above information, what are three important things you should note about Lindsay?

1. Has developmental delays; difficulty walking, cutting, holding a pencil, speaking, and understanding classroom content (fine- and gross-motor skills and cognitive/language delays).
2. Has no behavior problems; she likes music; she has delayed social skills; has difficulty initiating social contact with peers.
3. Began Hebrew phonics last year; learned and reviewed Hebrew letters one-on-one outside the classroom; is not expected to learn all the skills that other students are learning; the main goal of her learning is to have a positive Jewish experience.

What are your initial thoughts about how you might be able to help Lindsay successfully participate in some of her class activities?

Note: This question is presented to have participants begin thinking empathetically about working with a student with special needs. There are no correct answers to this question. Therefore, the instructor may need to guide participants to answer. If there is a silence longer than thirty seconds to a minute, ask participants to look back at their answers to the previous question and then make suggestions based on those answers. For instance, "She has trouble cutting." A participant may answer, "Whenever there are projects that involve cutting, I should be prepared to cut for her."

Wisdom from Our Sages

> Our Rabbis taught: A minor who knows how to shake the *lulav* is subject to the obligation of the *lulav*; [if he knows how] to wrap himself [in a tallit], he is subject to the obligation of *tzitzit*; [if he knows how] to lay *t'fillin*, his father must acquire *t'fillin* for him; if he is able to speak, his father must teach him Torah and the reading of the *Sh'ma*.
>
> Sukkah 42a
>
> Based on a translation in Ivan G. Marcus, *The Jewish Life Cycle: Rites of Passage from Biblical to Modern Times.*

After discussing the Wisdom from the Sages, pass out copies of learning plans (or the accommodations section of an IEP) to each student's assigned tzadik or tzadikah. If there are no learning plans or accommodations sections of IEPs to be distributed, share a basic profile of the student and his or her special needs verbally.

Thousands of years ago, our Sages taught in the Talmud about the obligation of children to perform the mitzvot of shaking the lulav on Sukkot, wearing a tallit and laying t'fillin, and learning Torah and reciting the Sh'ma.

At the end of the passage above, what is a child's father required to do if his child is able to speak? ____________

Refer to Workbook page 161

Does the text mention a particular age to begin teaching? ___________

How is this text different from what you have learned about the obligation to perform mitzvot beginning at the age of bar or bat mitzvah?

____

____

____

____

____

From this text we learn that we must teach Torah and mitzvot even to those who are not obligated to perform the commandments, no matter what their age. Likewise, just as we are obligated to teach Torah to our youngest children, so, too, we are obligated to teach Torah to every student.

The Talmud tells the story of Rabbi Peraida, who had to teach a student a lesson four hundred times before he understood it. During the teaching, Rabbi Peraida took a break to perform a mitzvah. When he returned to continue teaching the student the lesson four hundred times, the student explained that he could not understand it because of the interruption. Therefore, Rabbi Peraida started over again, teaching the student another four hundred times until he understood. Suddenly, a heavenly voice shouted out that Rabbi Peraida and his generation merited a place in the world-to-come. (from Eruvin 54b)

What do you learn from the story of Rabbi Peraida?_______________

____

____

____

____

____

____

Read a copy of your student's learning plan. If your supervisor does not have a written plan for you, he or she may provide you with information in a different way. Please take a moment to read the information that describes your student's specific special needs.

Refer to Workbook page 162

Use the space below to write down two or three facts about your student that you feel are important:

1. ____

2. ____

3. ____

4. ____

5. ____

Instruct participants to list two or three important facts about their student, just as they did for Lindsay earlier. Explain that they should only look to the introductory paragraph to find this information.

What questions do you have for your supervisor about your student?

1. ____

2. ____

3. ____

4. ____

5. ____

After participants complete the questions for the supervisor, take a moment to walk around the room and answer any questions. If there is a question for which you do not know the answer, be sure to tell the student that you will work to find the correct answer and share it with him or her in the coming days.

Prepare:

- Carefully study the classroom strategies and Hebrew strategies prior to the lesson and be prepared to demonstrate them.
- Have on hand examples of some of the materials described in the strategies, such as stickers and reward certificates, bendable wax sticks, pipecleaners, sticky notes (to cover portions of the textbook page), incentive/reward charts or pages, etc.
- Enlarge a sentence from a Hebrew prayer (*V'ahavta* is recommended), and make a copy for each participant.
- Provide each participant with something to be used as a pointer (a pencil, a Popsicle stick, etc.) and two different colors of highlighters (avoid red and green).

Notes:

- The "Understanding Classroom Strategies" and "Basic Strategies for Teaching Hebrew to Students with Learning Differences" sections are two of the most important in the curriculum. Therefore, you must carefully plan how to successfully teach these concepts, paying particular attention to the learning styles of the participants. Just as a learning plan is developed for students who learn differently, this is also an opportunity for modeling positive instructive techniques.
- Two creative ways of teaching this lesson are to preassign participants one or two of the strategies and then have them act out or demonstrate their strategy for the group, or have participants each read a rule and then demonstrate or explain how he or she could use it in class.
- Some suggested techniques to model are speaking slowly (strategy #1), pointing to the page and making body gestures during teaching (strategy #4), and clearly providing positive reinforcement after a participant answers a question (strategy #12).
- Regarding the use of praise, the best way to give positive reinforcement is to state the correct behavior without using a phrase such as I like. For example, the participant should state, "You're sitting so quietly, Johnny," rather than, "I like how you are sitting quietly, Johnny." This will place emphasis on the importance of the behavior.

Refer to Workbook page 163

WORKSHOP I

Part 3: Classroom Strategies for the Child Who Learns Differently

Objectives: By the end of this workshop, you will be able to:

- Understand a variety of classroom and individualized teaching strategies for teaching students with special needs.
- Identify specific strategies for your student's success in the classroom.
- Interpret and summarize the second part of your student's learning plan.
- Begin to model skills and behaviors for your student.

Understanding Classroom Strategies

Children with attention or processing difficulties, such as students with ADHD or an auditory processing disorder, have difficulty listening or paying attention in class. Certain learning disabilities also affect the ability to listen, as explained earlier. Now that you understand why these students have difficulty listening, you can begin to learn how to help them in class. The following are a list of classroom strategies to help children who have difficulty listening. These strategies will not be necessary for all children who learn differently, but they will generally be helpful if you are working with a student who has difficulty listening or focusing. As you begin working with your student, you should experiment with each of these strategies to see which works best.

1. Keep directions short and simple, and speak slowly.
2. Frequently repeat directions to the student.
3. Have the student repeat the directions back to you.
4. Use gestures (hand motions and body language) when providing directions.
5. Make sure that you and your student are sitting within close proximity of the teacher.
6. Use visuals whenever possible, such as writing directions down on paper as you say them or pointing to the word that the teacher is reading.
7. Give breaks often. If the student seems to be having problems focusing, allow him or her to take a break. Examples include taking a short walk or going to the library to read a book.
8. Review classroom rules with your student.
9. Use positive reinforcement. Create a positive reinforcement behavior management system using stars or happy faces. (Example, if Jamie gets

Refer to Workbook page 164

three stars by the end of Sunday school, he can visit the computer lab at the end of the day).

10. Show enthusiasm.
11. Don't fight the impossible. If hyperactivity is an issue for your student, simply ignore the child moving around or squirming in his or her seat.
12. Constantly offer praise. Comment on the student's positive behaviors as much as possible. Provide positive attention and positive reinforcement. Every child deserves praise each day!
13. Keep in mind that saying "sssh" is ineffective.
14. Use nonverbal cues to stop inappropriate behaviors (such as a nod, a tap on the shoulder, waving a finger, etc.).

Understanding Individualized Teaching Strategies for Hebrew Learning

Your student may have difficulty learning Hebrew for a variety of reasons. As a *tzadik* or *tzadikah,* you may be asked to work one-on-one with your student to help with Hebrew learning, and some *tzadikim* work as assistants providing Hebrew tutoring to a variety of students with learning differences, instead of working as classroom shadows.

Many students with special needs are not able to learn using traditional teaching methods. They may attend special schools or special education classes in their public schools. Many of these schools or classes provide specialized teaching for these children using multisensory teaching methods. This means that students may learn using their senses, such as tactile (touch) or visual (sight) cues.

- ***Empathy Challenge***

Read the following instructions and try to follow them exactly.

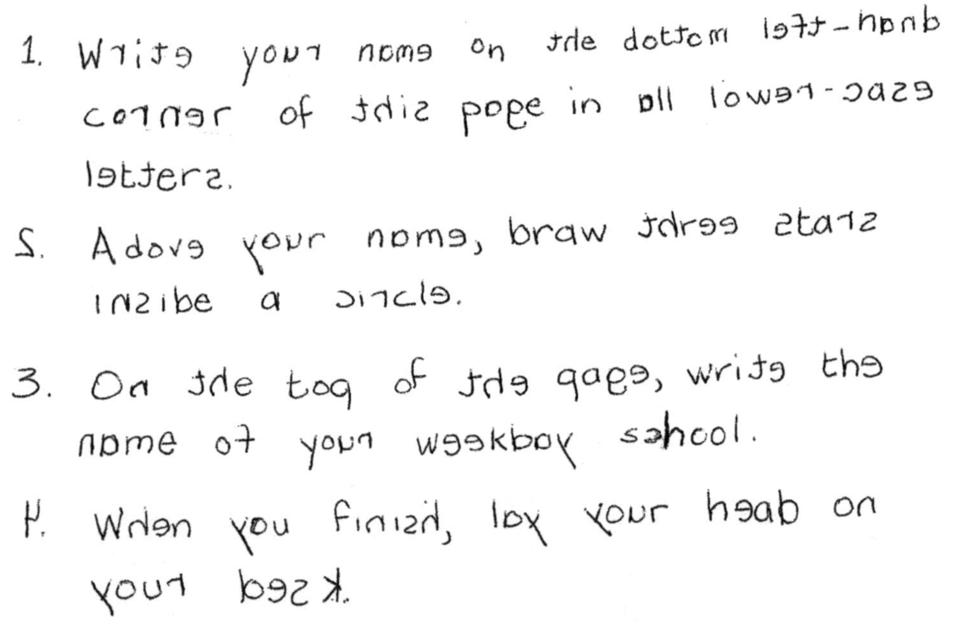

Follow-up Questions:

- Think back to some of your favorite teachers. Did they utilize any of these strategies? If so, which ones? Do you think they helped?
- Why do you think it is so important to praise students, especially those with special needs? (Oftentimes, students with special needs get very little praise during the week if they attend traditional schools; teachers and administrators sometimes communicate weaknesses clearly while rarely sharing positive feedback. The synagogue is one place where differences should be positively acknowledged or praised.)
- What challenges might you face with reward systems? (Rewards can be given out too often and lose meaning; students can become too focused on the reward and miss the meaning of the task.)

Notes:

- This empathy challenge is designed for participants to do individually.
- The empathy challenge will hopefully help participants understand how a child with dyslexia may see a written text. Students with dyslexia who have visual deficits often describe written texts as if the letters look like they are dancing around the page. Be sure to remind participants that this is just one example of how a text may look to a child and that not every child will see the text in the same way.

Refer to Workbook page 165

How did you feel when completing this activity and why?

How would you feel if you were asked to complete the directions above in a short amount of time? How would you feel if your teacher was angry with you for "not trying" after you were unable to complete the activity?

Learning Hebrew can be a challenge. When a child has a reading-based learning difference, learning Hebrew is even more challenging. The activity above gives you a brief experience of what these children deal with on a daily basis.

Basic Strategies for Teaching Hebrew to Students with Learning Differences

Here are some strategies that may be helpful to you when teaching Hebrew to a child who learns differently:

1. When teaching a letter that looks similar to another letter (e.g., *resh* and *dalet* or *chet* and *tav*), point out their similarities and differences by writing the letters side by side.
2. Have students use tactile exercises, such as molding the letters out of clay, pipe cleaners, or bendable wax sticks, so that they understand how the letters differ from each other.
3. Use fun mnemonic strategies (tricks to memorize) to help the student remember the sounds of letters and vowel sounds (such as the *resh* is more "rounded" than the *dalet*; its sound is *R*).
4. Enlarge the print size of the Hebrew text on a copy machine.
5. Remind your teacher not to call on students with reading-based learning differences to read out loud unless they volunteer.
6. Limit distractions from the page. (You can use self-adhesive notes to cover up pictures or other text on the sides of the page.)
7. Always have students read using their fingers or a pencil/pen to point to the words.

As you teach each Hebrew strategy, stop and demonstrate the strategy with examples:

- Draw a *dalet* and a *resh* on the whiteboard or flip chart and circle some of the different parts of the letters (like the line that continues on the top right of a *dalet*).
- Provide participants with a pipe cleaner or bendable wax stick and ask them to form a letter that you draw on the board.
- Have participants create mnemonics for some letters (such as a *bet* has a "bar at the bottom" or a "belly button").
- Show participants a text or a line from a prayer that is enlarged on a photocopier and explain that the enlargement makes it easier for students to see the dots and vowels.
- Ask: "Why do you think it is important not to call on students with reading-based learning differences unless they volunteer? " (to avoid causing them embarrassment)
- Demonstrate how to minimize distractions on a page by covering up parts of the text with sticky notes.
- Have students use their pointers to follow along as you read.

Refer to Workbook page 166

8. Segment (or break apart) syllables for the student. An ideal way to do this is by highlighting each syllable in alternating colors, as below:

בָּרוּךְ אַתָּה, יְיָ אֱלֹהֵינוּ, מֶלֶךְ הָעוֹלָם,
יוֹצֵר אוֹר וּבוֹרֵא חֹשֶׁךְ,

9. Provide simplified transliteration when appropriate. (For example, in *V'ahavta*, the word (insert Hebrew word here) is a tricky combination of sounds, so you may choose to write "*uv'shoch'b'ch*" above the text.)

- ***Empathy Challenge***

Read the following starting from the black arrow at the bottom left and then continuing going down from the white arrow. Then, continue reading alternating going up and down.

e	w	a	n	r	e		t	e	r
r		m	y	d	n	g	o	v	y
b	c			l		n			
e	a	o	p	i	a	i	l	e	f
H	n	t	e	h	n	y	e	h	i
			o	c	d	r	a	t	r
g	b	g	p			t	r		s
n	e	n	l	g	e		n	r	t
l		i	e	n	v	s		o	
d	c	g		i	e	t	H	f	t
a	h	n	i	d	n	l	e		i
e	a	e	n	u		u	b	w	m
R	l	l	c	l	a	d	r	e	e.

Prepare:

- Before facilitating this exercise, be sure to follow the directions when doing it on your own. On the first read, hold your hands behind your back when reading the text. On the second read, use your finger or some type of pointer to help your eyes track the text.
- After participating in this challenge, many teachers have made it a point to make all their students, regardless of their learning style, track their Hebrew reading with their fingers or a pointer.

- Pass out an enlarged copy of a Hebrew text (a verse from *V'ahavta* is recommended) and ask participants to practice highlighting the Hebrew syllables by alternating colored highlighters. Using this technique is more effective than breaking apart syllables with pencil lines. Alternating colors helps those with visual processing deficits and reading-based learning disabilities track from right to left with greater ease.
- Highlighting *shva'im* can be a bit confusing.

As a rule of thumb, one-syllable words, such as et, should be highlighted in one color only. When a shva is under the first letter of a word, the short/stop sound that it makes is counted as a syllable and *tzadikim* should be instructed to highlight it in its own color. Additionally, when two *shva'im* are found side by side in a word, the letter (beginning the complete syllable) above the second shva should also be highlighted in its own color. Other cases of *shva'im* are mostly silent and are highlighted together with the preceding vowel and letter. The word *Adonai* should be circled to remind students that its pronunciation should be memorized. Even though there are other specific and complex grammatical rules with shva'im, it is not necessary to get too bogged down with them. As participants are working, the instructor should circle the room to be sure participants have grasped the concept, since this technique is one of the keys to teaching students who learn differently to read Hebrew.

- Be careful not to write the transliteration from left to right above long words. Instead, write each individual syllable's transliteration above the particular highlighted syllable. Demonstrate this on the whiteboard or flip chart. This method will allow the student to read the Hebrew word from right to left.

Now reread the above, this time using your finger to point to the words that you are trying to read to help you follow along.

Which time did you find it easier to read and understand the sentence above—using your finger or without using your finger? Why?

Most participants will answer "with my finger." The reason is that a finger or a pointer helps students' eyes focus on the upcoming letters and prevents them from skipping letters or losing their place

Explain how using a simple strategy can have a major impact on your ability to accomplish something basic.

This question can produce a variety of responses. A simple answer is "Strategies provide us with tools to help us learn a new skill."

Applying What You Learned

Remember Lindsay's learning plan (Part 1) from page 159? Take a minute to look back over this information.

What learning differences does Lindsay have? Developmental delays (difficulties walking, cutting, holding a pencil, speaking, and understanding classroom content).

Before reading Part 2 of her learning plan, discuss as a group what strategies you think might be effective for Lindsay.

Refer to Workbook page 168

LEARNING PLAN FOR LINDSAY (PART 2)

1. Lindsay will be provided with a special needs teaching assistant (from our *tzadikim* program) in class.
2. Both the teacher and the teaching assistant will help Lindsay with simple social exchanges with peers and her teacher.
3. Lindsay will be assisted with all classroom activities. The teacher and *tzadik(ah)* will help simplify those activities so Lindsay can participate. Alternative activities will be available (i.e., coloring pictures with a Judaic theme), if needed. During Hebrew time, she may go to the library to work one-on-one with her *tzadik(ah)*.
4. If needed as a behavioral distraction, Lindsay will be taken out of the class to walk around with her *tzadik(ah)* for approximately five to ten minutes. She will then come back to class and again participate.
5. The *tzadik(ah)* will provide one-on-one Hebrew instruction, utilizing the following strategies:
   - Limit distractions from the page.
   - Always have Lindsay read using her finger or a pencil/pen to point to the words.
   - Segment (or break apart) syllables.
6. Periods of time without the *tzadik(ah)* sitting next to her (such as during music or another engaging activity) should be attempted as appropriate.
7. The teacher/parents will call the learning consultant at any time during the school year if problems arise.

Notes:

- The goal of this exercise is for participants to try to apply some of the strategies presented in the workshop. This is a difficult exercise. However, it will challenge participants to look back at the strategies presented and think about them in a practical way.
- After participants answer the first question, ask them to flip back to the two sets of strategies provided on pages 163 and 164. As a group, they should decide which of these would be helpful for Lindsay. For example, the first six classroom strategies would all be helpful because she has difficulties understanding classroom content.

Wisdom from Our Sages

Human dignity is so important that it supersedes even a biblical prohibition.

Berachot 19b

What do you think this text from the Talmud means?

As you have been learning throughout this workshop, a major part of your job as a *tzadik(ah)* is to help your student feel "the same" as all other students in the school. In school settings, this is called "inclusion." Inclusion is a philosophy that all types of learners (including those with special needs) can be taught in the same classroom.

Judaism has always taught respect for others. Almost two thousand years ago, the Rabbis already began teaching the importance of preserving another human's dignity (in Hebrew this is called *kavod ha'briut*). *Kavod ha'briut* was so important to them that the ruling was made that one could break a law from the Torah in order to protect another person from embarrassment.

There can be many different answers here. For example, if someone had a drug or alcohol addiction and had to be hospitalized, we may lie and say that the person was suffering from something else so as to not cause him or her any embarrassment.

Can you think of a Jewish law that may need to be broken in order to protect someone's dignity? ____________________

Have you ever wondered why saying the blessing before and after the Torah reading is called an *aliyah* and not the act of reading the Torah itself? The Rabbis knew that most people do not have the skills to read or chant Torah, so they appoint permanent readers for the text itself and then honor those who bless the reading. This is another form of *kavod ha'briut,* or avoiding embarrassment of others.

What simple acts of kavod ha'briut can you do to help your student avoid embarrassment? Keep my finger on the page while the teacher was reading so the student can always find the right place; prepare some of the work for the student, such as cutting out the different shapes, repeat directions slowly so that the student will know exactly what to do next.

Refer to Workbook page 170

Understanding Strategies Needed to Help the Student You Will Be Mentoring

You have been given a learning plan or other information about the student you will be shadowing. Depending on what exactly your supervisor gave you, you may or may not have a list of strategies (similar to the format used for Lindsay above) to use with your student. If you have been given a specific learning plan, rewrite the strategies for your student now in your own words to help you better understand what you will be doing. If you have not been given specific strategies, use this as an opportunity to write your own learning plan, using the strategies outlined in this book and taking into consideration your student's specific special need.

- If you are providing the information orally, we recommend organizing your strategies on the sample below (three blank plans have been provided). Then, present them to the *tzadikim* one by one and discuss them as you go. Encourage the participants to write the strategies in their own words.
- Regardless of which way plans are presented to the *tzadikim*, the facilitator should prepare some examples of how *tzadikim* can model skills and behaviors for each of the students with special needs.

Learning Plan Strategies for ________________ [your student's name]

1. ______________________________

2. ______________________________

3. ______________________________

4. ______________________________

5. ______________________________

6. ______________________________

7. ______________________________

8. ______________________________

List three ways you can model skills and behaviors for your student.

1. ______________________________

2. ______________________________

3. ______________________________

Refer to Workbook page 171

Reward Chart for ______________________________ [your student's name]

Tefilah	Hebrew Lesson	Music	Torah Lesson	Art

I earned ______ stars today!

Additional Comments: ____

____

____

Workshop II: Facilitating the Curriculum

The second workshop session should take place at the end of the first month of school or three or four weeks after the *tzadikim* have begun working with their students. Because the school year is in full swing at the time of this workshop, the learning consultant should be aware that *tzadikim* are busy getting used to their own school schedules and homework. Accordingly, it is a good idea to send several reminders about the meeting, its location, and the self-study exercises. Students typically come with a lot of concerns and questions about their work. Therefore, the instructor's main goal is to reassure *tzadikim* that working with special needs students is not easy and to answer any pressing questions they may have at this point.

The last exercise in their preparatory work instructs the *tzadikim* to come prepared with questions they have for their supervisor. In between the first and second session, the supervisor should be observing and taking notes about the performance of the *tzadikim*. When a supervisor finds specific issues with one *tzadik* or *tzadikah*, in particular, he or she should meet one-on-one with him or her. In rare instances, if a *tzadik* or *tzadikah* is not meeting program goals, he or she should be given additional and specific directions for necessary steps to succeed in the program.

Notes:

- Start the workshop with a mixer or an icebreaker. Kinesthetic icebreakers are a great way to energize your group. Two suggested icebreakers are: "Silent Lineup," where participants are asked to line up by birthday, height, etc. without talking, and "Machines," where participants are broken up into two groups and are assigned a machine to act out (such as a record player, a toaster, or a DVD player).

WORKSHOP II

Self-Study Exercises

(to be completed prior to attending Workshop II)

By now you have had some time to get to know the student with whom you are working. At the last session, you were given a piece of paper with a description of a child with special needs. When you met the student you were assigned to shadow, however, you began to see a real person with feelings and emotions, not just words on a page.

Before your meeting, what did you expect your student to be like?

____

____

____

____

____

The fill-in-the-blank questions in this section are straightforward and should not have been difficult for participants to answer.

What were some of the differences from your expectations?

____

____

____

____

____

On your first day with your student, what were some of the hardest things for you? ____

____

____

____

____

____

What things were surprisingly easy? ______________________

____

____

____

____

____

Ask participants to share their answers to the questions with the group. It is not necessary for each participant to share every one of their answers Acknowledge all responses positively with a nod, a gesture, or a one- or two-word answer.

Look back a couple of pages and review some of the suggested strategies for working with your student. Which of these strategies worked well? Which did not work well?

Strategies that worked well: ______________________

____

____

____

____

____

Strategies that did not work so well: ______________________

____

____

____

____

____

As participants share the strategies that did not work well, explain that these strategies often take practice. Strategies like these don't always work the first time, but over time these strategies may succeed. Encourage participants to continue trying these strategies so they can be reassessed at the next meeting.

In the time you have spent with your student, we hope that you have been able to connect with some of his or her feelings and emotions. Though sometimes it is hard to relate to someone so different from us, when we are in the role of caregiver, we typically connect with that person more easily. Like a parent relating to a child, the more we help someone, the less we come to see his or her differences.

Martin Buber, one of the greatest Jewish theologians of the twentieth century, spoke of two types of relationships: I-It and I-Thou. I-It relationships are basically those exchanges we have every day with store clerks, waiters, and others. They

Ask:

- "The end of this self-study presented a new way to look at relationships, as taught by Martin Buber. In the time that you have spent with your student, would you say you have established a good relationship or have you found it difficult to make a connection?" Allow students to answer this question honestly without any interruptions. It is important for *tzadikim* to voice their feelings.
- If participants share difficulties, ask: "What are some of the barriers or issues that are making the start of your relationship so difficult?" Acknowledge all responses and take notes when necessary. If a *tzadik(ah)* has a particular issue, tell him or her that you will digest the situation and make additional recommendations soon.

are characterized by a common need or a relationship of utility. For example, when I have finished picking out all my groceries, I go to the register and pay for them. The clerk rings them up and we have a brief conversation, yet it is typically a shallow conversation (characterized by remarks such as "It's really hot today" or "I can't believe the price of milk these days").

I-Thou relationships, on the other hand, are relationships between two people who care for each other. This can be with parents, a girlfriend or boyfriend, or even a teacher. In these encounters, both people care for the other person's welfare and needs, and both people fully accept each other. We think of these relationships as genuine.

Buber goes on to teach that when we have true I-Thou relationships, when both parties genuinely care for each other, God is present in the relationship and in these relationships, we can discover God.

Though you have only recently met your student, you are creating a caring relationship, similar to an I-Thou relationship. Do you feel a special connection to your student? If so, how does this make you feel? And, if not, what are some of the barriers that are keeping you from creating these special connections?

____

____

____

____

____

Closing Questions:

Allow participants to ask any questions that they wrote down. If you can give simple answers to their questions, do so immediately. If they ask complex questions or questions that apply only to one particular *tzadik* or *tzadikah*, tell him or her that you will answer the questions at the end of the session or one-on-one.

Before you forget, do you have any questions that you would like to ask your supervisor at the next session? Quickly jot them down.

1. ____________________________________

2. ____________________________________

3. ____________________________________

Notes

Refer to Workbook page 179

Before dividing the class into groups and beginning the case studies, ask:

- "If your parents told you tonight at dinner that they are going to take you out of your current school tomorrow and start you in a new one, how would you advocate for yourself?" (Possible answers: "I would tell them I'm not going," "I would ask why they want me to change," etc.)
- "If a group of your friends started teasing and then beating up a smaller student in the grade below you and you didn't like it, how would you advocate for that teen?"(Possible answers: "I would tell them to stop," "I would tella teacher or counselor," etc.)

In the introduction of the book, we learned of the rabbi's brilliance as he advocated for the boy who thought he was a chicken. Though your audience may not come up with such creative strategies, the opening case studies are vehicles to see how thoughtful your students can be. Encourage *tzadikim* to stretch their minds to come up with the most creative solutions for these case studie

WORKSHOP II

The Invisible Need: Becoming a Classroom Advocate

Objectives: By the end of this workshop, you will be able to:

- Understand the importance of advocating for your student.
- Assist teachers in differentiating between behavioral needs and learning needs.
- Recognize additional learning needs in the classroom and be proactive in assisting the teacher.

Understanding the Importance of Advocating for Your Student

Now that you have had a couple of weeks of experience in the classroom, you have become acquainted with your student and some of his or her needs. In some of the challenging situations, you may have noticed that traditional teaching or classroom management does not work. At those junctures, you may have found strategies (like the ones you learned in the first workshop session) that work well. When you utilize the techniques on your learning plan or your own strategies, you are advocating for your student.

An advocate is someone who stands up or speaks out for the good of someone or something. Although you are becoming aware of and used to your student's special needs, the behaviors that he or she displays may be deemed inappropriate to the outside world. The more you work with your student, the more you are learning how to intervene when necessary. The next exercise is designed to help you become more comfortable with your new role as an advocate and to practice taking on this new role in other situations.

- ***Empathy Challenge: Advocating in Various Situations***

Divide up into three groups. Each group should take one of the three case studies below and answer the questions as a group. Pick a spokesperson and prepare to present your findings to the larger group.

Refer to Workbook page 180

Case Study 1

Note: In the following two examples, one of the goals is for *tzadikim* to empathize with these students by practicing listening to the frustrated child's feelings and then repeating them back.

You are David's *tzadik* or *tzadikah*. David's Judaics teacher, Mrs. Cohen, has an intense lesson plan today. The children are reading from the text for a prolonged period and she is calling on different readers. The children are asked to sit quietly and wait for their turn to read. Mrs. Cohen is speaking in a monotone voice and is not introducing any new activities. Some of the students are laying their heads down on the desk, some are twirling their pencils or doodling, and others are staring off into space. A few are listening intently. David is fidgeting in his seat and keeps standing up and sitting down. At one point he gets up and walks around his desk in two circles, but then decides to sit back down. He soon begins to make funny noises that are distracting the students around him.

How would you feel sitting in Mrs. Cohen's classroom?

bored, tired, not engaged.

What are some things going on in the classroom that may be making it difficult for David to sit quietly?

Teachers is spending too much time with students privately and ignoring the rest of the class.

The teacher is not teaching anything new.

The children are sitting for long periods of time.

If Mrs. Cohen were your student's teacher, we would recommend that you share some of David's difficulties in her class with your supervisor. What would you report to him or her?

The teacher expects David to sit for long periods of time and listen to other students read. David needs to change activities more often and be allowed to take breaks when others are reading for long periods.

Refer to Workbook page 181

Case Study 2

You are Kayla's *tzadik* or *tzadikah*. Today Kayla's class is learning about Israel. Her teacher, Mr. Jacobs, loves to play a game called "Around the World." In this game, two students are asked to stand up at one time. Then they are asked a question about Israel. In order to move on to the next round of the game, one student must correctly answer the question before the other student. Kayla has played this game for the past two weeks and she always answers her questions incorrectly, so she doesn't advance. Today, when Mr. Jacobs announces that they are about to play the game, all the children in the class seem happy to play except for Kayla. She tells you that she needs to go to the bathroom. She seems very upset, so you go with her. As soon as she gets outside the classroom, Kayla starts to cry and says to you, "I hate this game. I never know the right answer because I'm so stupid. I don't want to go back to class."

If you were to ask Kayla how she is feeling in this class, what do you think she would say?

"I feel stupid when we play this game." "I hate this game/class," "I am mad at Mr. Jacobs."

What are some of the things that make this game so frustrating for Kayla?

1. reading out loud.
2. feeling pressured or the competition.
3. feeling incapable.

If Mr. Jacobs were your student's teacher, we would recommend that you share some of Kayla's difficulties in his class with your supervisor. What would you report to him or her? (Some possible answers) Kayla should not have to play knowledge-based games. If she is going to play the game, Kayla should be given the answer first so that she can feel good about what she has learned. Kayla should be allowed to answer a question by herself without having to compete with another student. .

Refer to Workbook page 182

Case Study 3

You are Dylan's *tzadik* or *tzadikah*. Dylan loves the Judaics class, but when it is time for Hebrew, he becomes very anxious. His teacher, Ms. Hirsh, randomly calls on students to read out loud. Although Dylan's learning plan specifies that she not call on Dylan to read aloud in class because of his dyslexia, she seems to always forget. When Dylan is called on, the other students often laugh at him because he cannot recognize the letters and the teacher has to practically sound out the entire word for him. After class today, Dylan says to you, "I wish I was smart like the rest of the kids. I want to be able to read, too. I heard them laughing at me today!"

If you were to ask Dylan how he is feeling in this class, what do you think he would say?

I feel crummy because I am so stupid

What are some of the things that make this class frustrating for Dylan?

His teacher forgets his need and makes him read Hebrew out loud.

Dylan has trouble reading Hebrew

When Dylan reads out loud, the other children laugh at him.

If Ms. Hirsh were your student's teacher, we would recommend that you share some of Dylan's difficulties in her class with your supervisor. What would you report to him or her?

Refer to Workbook page 183

Wisdom from Our Sages

> All of Israel is responsible for one another.
>
> Shavuot 39a

Although this short text from the Talmud seems simple, it has many different meanings in different contexts. Let's take it apart to better understand it. In Hebrew, the text reads Kol Yisrael (all of Israel). Who or what does "all of Israel" refer to? ______________________

Jews all over the world, and in the context of this course, it could include those with special needs and disabilities.

In what ways are we, as Jews, responsible for one another? List at least five examples.

We take care of the poor by giving *tzedakah*. We take care of our Jewish brothers and sisters in other countries who are persecuted by bringing them to Israel. We give to Israel to take care of our people who live there. If someone were teasing another Jewish kid in our school we should stick up for him. We volunteer for Jewish organizations. Our Israeli brothers and sisters serve in the IDF to protect the State of Israel. We give money to Jewish organizations to maintain them for the next generations.

In Midrash Raba (Vayikra 4:6), the Rabbis tell the story of a man who is sitting in a boat with others. Suddenly, he takes out a hand drill and begins boring a hole in the bottom of the boat. When someone on the boat asks him what he is doing, he shrugs the man off, stating, "It's really none of your business." The man replies, "If the water begins to fill up our boat and we sink, not only will you go down, but we will all go down with you."

Refer to Workbook page 184

Looking more globally at our responsibility as Jews to help others, how might this story be compared to the work that you do as a tzadik(ah)?

The person in the boat was just looking out for himself. This teaches, that in life, we have to take care of each other and not just look out for ourselves. The children we work with cannot always take care of themselves, so we have to step up and look out for them, too (so they won't drown)

Differentiating between Behavioral and Learning Needs

As an advocate for a child with attention or processing issues, you now know how his or her actions may often seem like true, intentional misbehaviors, rather than an actual inability to listen and comprehend what the teacher wants him or her to understand. Sometimes, however, you may be working with a child who displays poor behavioral choices and is utilizing a behavior management system such as those discussed in Workshop I (i.e., a star chart). It is important for you to continue to clearly understand the difference between a learning need and a behavioral need so you are able to properly employ the right strategy for the child with whom you are working. For example, if you are working with a child who is unable to follow lengthy instructions, due to attention or processing issues, and his or her teacher is constantly yelling at him or her for not listening, this is a clear example of a teacher not understanding the nature of the student's learning difference and genuine inability to understand and follow the teacher's instructions.

Note: The next section helps students differentiate between common behaviors and special needs. As you present this section, remind participants that many behavioral issues are a product of a learning difference. Therefore, sometimes the line between learning issues and behavioral needs is blurry. However, there are some clear cut cases. As participants discuss their answers, be sure to listen to the explanation before stating whether it is right or wrong. If the explanation makes sense, acknowledge the good reasoning and then present another (or the correct) answer to the question.

Think back to Workshop I. What were some strategies you learned to help a child with learning needs? List three below:

1. ____

2. ____

3. ____

Participants may choose any three strategies from pages 163 and 164 from the *tzadikim* guide.)

Refer to Workbook page 185

Now consider specific strategies used for children with behavioral issues:

1. (Strategies 5, 7, 8, 9, 13, and 14 from pages 163 and 164 would all be good answers.

2. However, because there is such a fine line here, almost any strategy is okay.)

3. ______________________________

Note: Remind *tzadikim* that, as advocates, they should be the first to educate others that the student is not "bad," but rather the behavior may stem from an issue that may need to be addressed. Some examples of those issues may be that the instructions were not clear and simple or there were not enough breaks provided for this student during the lesson.

Is it possible for some of these to overlap? Your answer should be yes! Many of the strategies that we learned in Workshop I can be applied to a child with both learning and behavioral needs. What is important to understand here, again, is your critical role as an advocate. We want to prevent, whenever possible, and intervene, when necessary, when our student's actions are being attributed solely to that fact that the student is "bad" or is constantly "not listening and misbehaving." We also want to help the teacher understand that we are dealing with a child who has very real issues listening and understanding what is being said to him or her.

Below is a list of events that may occur on a typical day with a child who learns differently. As you read through them, consider if each action displayed below reflects a behavioral or a learning need. Circle the one that you feel fits best or is more likely the better answer for each situation. You are not given full information on each item, so be creative and use your best judgment when deciding what you think may really be causing each student's actions.

Answers:

Note: Remember that we are seeking the best answer to each question in this exercise and that many answers could be interchangeable. However, there are clues given (highlighted in parentheses below) that should lead students to the correct answer.

1. Learning need (has dyslexia)

1. Jason has dyslexia and is embarrassed to read aloud. He refuses to read out loud when the teacher calls on him.

   LEARNING NEED BEHAVIORAL NEED

2. Behavioral need (forgot . . . not prepared . . . left her book at home)

2. Anna tells the teacher she doesn't want to read aloud because she forgot to do her homework over the last three weeks and she is additionally not prepared because she left her book at home.

   LEARNING NEED BEHAVIORAL NEED

3. Behavioral need (substitute teacher . . . because he thinks it's funny)

3. Mark tells the substitute teacher that his name is Max because he thinks it's funny.

   LEARNING NEED BEHAVIORAL NEED

Refer to Workbook page 186

4. Lisa sits down and is the only one in class not participating in the art project because she cannot remember all the steps the teacher explained.

   LEARNING NEED BEHAVIORAL NEED

5. Mark, who is sitting in the desk behind Janie, knows that the teacher told him to mold his clay into a rectangle for the mezuzah art project, but he instead makes small little balls of clay which he is happily placing in Janie's long braid.

   LEARNING NEED BEHAVIORAL NEED

6. The teacher asks the class to open their books to page 9, complete numbers 1 through 5 at the top of the page, and then lay their heads down on their desks when they are done. Jason opens his book to page 5 and lays his head on the desk.

   LEARNING NEED BEHAVIORAL NEED

7. Mrs. Cohen tells Beth five times that a *resh* has a rounded edge and a *dalet* doesn't, but Beth continues to confuse them every time she tries to read a word with either letter.

   LEARNING NEED BEHAVIORAL NEED

8. Kevin's teacher keeps asking him to sit still in his seat, but he continues to wiggle in his chair.

   LEARNING NEED BEHAVIORAL NEED

9. Lawrence thinks it is funny to chew gum in class and then place his chewed gum under the desk when the teacher isn't looking.

   LEARNING NEED BEHAVIORAL NEED

10. Eric is trying to write the Hebrew word *Shabbat*, but his *bet* looks like a *tav*, and his *shin* looks more like an ant crawling with three legs. His friend sitting next to him laughs because he thinks Eric is trying to be funny by drawing the letters looking so "silly."

    LEARNING NEED BEHAVIORAL NEED

Answers:

4. Learning need (cannot remember all the steps the teacher explained)

5. Behavioral need (knows that thebteacher told him to)

6. Learning need (There are so many directions and Jason misses them.)

7. Learning need (continues to confuse them)

8. Learning need (keeps asking him to sit . . . he continues to wiggle)

9. Behavioral need (thinks it is funny)

10. Learning need (trying to write)

Refer to Workbook page 187

Notes:

- There are so many different types of learners in each classroom and it is difficult for teachers to differentiate between students who are acting out for attention or because they have some type of special need. Because tzadikim are being trained in special needs, we can use them "in the trenches" to identify other students who may be having trouble learning, concentrating or causing disruptions in the classroom.2 Though *tzadikim* are not experts, they quickly learn to recognize these challenges.
- The next exercise is designed to train *tzadikim* to know what to do when they witness other learning issues in the classroom.
- The answers to the following five questions are unpacked and explained in the next section in the *tzadikim* guide.

Review your answers as a group and discuss them. Discuss what really might be causing each of the students to display the behaviors described above.

Recognizing Additional Learning Needs in the Classroom

As you are learning to be an advocate for a child who learns differently, what happens when you notice another child in the same class who is displaying many of the behaviors that you learned about in Workshop I? If you are clearly noticing needs for this child, what happens when the teacher misses these needs? What happens if this child is constantly being reprimanded by the teacher, and you feel that there may be something else going on that is causing this child to constantly misbehave in the eyes of his or her teacher? What do you do? Can you advocate for another child with suspected learning needs? The answer is yes! However, you must be very careful to go through the proper avenues when trying to facilitate a positive change for the child you have been observing.

Below is a list of possible actions that you may take. Based on what you have learned until now, after each statement write "true" if you believe the statement describes an appropriate action for you as a tzadik(ah) to take, or write "false" if it does not.

Use the strategies suggested in your student's learning plan to write a learning plan for the other student in your class. Present the learning plan to the teacher. ____________________

Ask your rabbi, educator, or supervisor to come and observe the child in class. ____________________

When the child is having trouble concentrating, take the initiative to take the other student outside for a walk in order to give him a break (since you know this works well for your student). ____________________

Ask the teacher if you can talk to him or her after class about what you are noticing with this child and some things that you think you might be able to do to help. Ask if you can try to help. ____________________

Find that child's parents and ask them if their child has a special need.

____

Refer to Workbook page 188

Now let's take a look at these questions more carefully:

Answers:

1. As you have probably come to realize, your learning consultant spends a lot of time writing learning plans for each student with special needs. He or she has particular expertise in special needs and education. The longer you work as *tzadik or tzadikah*, the more familiar you will become with certain special needs and strategies to assist students. However, it is important to rely on the expertise of the learning consultant to make the larger decisions for students in your school. — 1. Bad Option

2. Whenever you notice something that doesn't feel comfortable in your classroom, as an advocate for students you have the right and responsibility to point it out to the administration. When this occurs, you should first think about who the best person to contact is. Usually, you should speak to your learning consultant. Sometimes, he or she sees the same issue, but has determined that it is not necessary to correct at that time. — 2. Good Option

3. Even though you have learned successful strategies for your own student, it is important to remember that your teacher is the ultimate authority in your classroom. Though it is always helpful to share successful strategies with your teacher, be careful to respect proper boundaries with your teacher. — 3. Good Option

4. You have been given many tools for assisting students. Though teachers are typically trained in classroom management, often they cannot see what you observe as a second leader in the classroom. Sharing strategies in a respectful manner with your teacher is helpful to your school. — 4. Good Option

5. You should always remember that it is the learning consultant's job to discuss special needs with parents. Though you feel it may be helpful to share information with other parents, there are many legal issues that go along with sharing too much information. Speaking with another parent is not your role as a *tzadik or tzadikah*. — 5. Bad Option

Congratulations! You are now another key advocate for your student and for other children at your synagogue who may also have special needs. Remember how important this role is. Your student is able to have a meaningful and positive Jewish experience because of what you are doing to help him or her succeed in the classroom. Hopefully, you are starting to develop a strong I-Thou relationship with your student as well.

Refer to Workbook page 189

WORKSHOP III

Self-Study Exercises

(to be completed prior to attending Workshop III)

Have you ever counted the days waiting for something exciting, only to become disappointed when that time arrives? Sometimes, our expectations do not live up to reality. So, too, reality sets in the more you work with your student.

As the months have passed and you and your student have become familiar with each other's ways, hopefully a positive routine has developed. Though a plan has been set out for you, even the best strategies do not always produce the most effective results.

Describe a situation in which you knew you helped your student.

Describe your feelings when you succeeded.

The third workshop is designed as a midyear reflection and should be conducted just before winter break. By the middle of the year, *tzadikim* typically establish a successful daily pattern for working with their students. As the *tzadikim's* supervisor, the learning consultant should be regularly checking in with the tzadikim to make sure that they are utilizing the suggested strategies for their students. However, the *tzadikim* will be the best evaluators of the strategies and if the strategies are working for their students. This workshop focuses on helping *tzadikim* evaluate the suggested strategies.

Even though a *tzadik(ah)* may claim a strategy is not working, the learning consultant must work in partnership with him or her to determine if the strategy is truly ineffective. In this workshop, the facilitator should spend ample time teaching the TASC method (page xx in the *tzadikim* guide) to *tzadikim*, emphasizing the importance of exhausting all options before giving up on a particular strategy the *tzadik(ah)* deems to be ineffective. Sometimes it is not the strategy that fails, but rather the person attempting to implement it. Therefore, the facilitator should also be careful not to abandon a strategy without first working through it with the *tzadik(ah)*. The role-playing situations at the end of the chapter should help reinforce the process and assist *tzadikim* in tweaking strategies and making minor adjustments, as necessary.

Notes:

- Because these questions may require difficult reflections for participants, be sure to positively acknowledge all answers. Additionally, you may want to point out some of the positive interactions between *tzadikim* and their students that you have witnessed over the past few months.
- Remember that the *tzadikim* are the ones in the trenches and that even though most of these strategies are tried-and true, *tzadikim* are entitled to their own feelings about their interactions. Reassure them when reassurance is warranted and also make polite suggestions when they fail.

Refer to Workbook page 190

Describe a situation when you feel your assistance did not work.

Describe your feelings when you feel you failed.

Prepare:

- Additional copies of student learning plans (or whatever was provided at Workshop I)
- A package of foil star stickers
- The instructor should write the word TASC on the whiteboard or flip chart with the acrostic below:

T ry the strategy again, even if it fails the first few times.
A sk your supervisor or teacher for help.
S hare the techniques that have been successful.
C ollaborate to find a new strategy.

- Make a copy of the role-playing scenarios (Appendix H) and then cut them out to be distributed to pairs during the workshop.

At the outset, ask: "Before we begin our lesson, are there any questions or topics that you feel are important to address during this session about your work or your student?" If there are complex questions or questions that apply only to one particular participant, tell the *tzadik* or *tzadikah* that you will answer his or her questions at the end of the session or one-on-one. If they ask simple logistical questions or questions important to answer before the main discussion, take a few minutes to do so. If they ask questions to which you do not have the answer, tell the participants that you will work on finding the answers after this session and get back to them.

Notes:

- Pass out a new copy of the learning plan or ask students to look back at the learning plan strategies they wrote down on page 185 (in their *tzadikim* guides). Hand out a page or a section of foil star stickers.
- After asking *tzadikim* to place stickers next to strategies that they use consistently, ask participants to write the answer to the question.
- Working in pairs, ask participants to share with their partner a situation when they used a specific strategy that was successful and why they believe it was successful. Circulate around the room to listen to some of the success stories.
- Collect the copies of the learning plans at the end of this exercise to be used in Workshop IV.

Refer to Workbook page 191

WORKSHOP III

Reevaluating Your Student's Needs

Objectives: By the end of this workshop, you will be able to:

- Evaluate the success of current teaching strategies.
- Understand the steps to take when certain strategies in a learning plan are no longer successful.
- Understand that the learning needs of students change often as they mature.
- Apply new learning strategies in consultation with the learning consultant/educational director as needed (the "TASC" plan).

Evaluating the Success of Current Teaching Strategies

At the beginning of this program, you must have been overwhelmed by your new responsibility. You were given information about a student with special needs and a learning plan (or you had to develop your own), and then you were thrust into a classroom to assist your student in adjusting to a new classroom situation. Now that half of the school year is almost over, it is time to take a step back and see how things are progressing. Is your student's learning plan still meeting his or her needs? Are all the classroom modifications still necessary? Have you experimented with different techniques, or sought assistance from others? This workshop is designed to help you through the process of evaluating your student's learning plan.

Learning Plan Evaluation Exercise

In order to complete this exercise, you are going to need a copy of your student's learning plan and some foil star stickers. Quickly reread through the learning plan. Then go back and place a star sticker next to each strategy that you are still using consistently with your student.

Which strategy, in particular, do you find most helpful and why? ______

______

______

______

______

______

Refer to Workbook page 192

Now, pair up with another *tzadik(ah)*. Share with him or her a specific classroom situation in which you used this strategy noted on your classroom learning plan and how the strategy was successful. Explain how you feel your student benefited from this intervention.

Wisdom from Our Sages

Note: One of the overall goals of the tzadikim program is to develop student leadership skills. This text study focuses on the skill of sharing responsibilities.

Moses sat as a magistrate among the people, while the people stood around Moses from morning until evening. But when Moses's father-in-law [Jethro] saw how much Moses had to do for the people, he said, "What is this thing that you are doing to the people? Why do you act alone, while all the people stand around you from morning until evening?"

Exodus 18:13–15

Moses's father-in-law said to him, "The thing you are doing is not right; you will surely wear yourself out, and these people as well. For the task is too heavy for you—you cannot do it alone."

Exodus 18:17–18

You shall also seek out from among all the people capable men who fear God, trustworthy men who spurn ill-gotten gain. Set these over them as chiefs of thousands, hundreds, fifties, and tens, and let them judge the people at all times. Have them bring every major dispute to you, but let them decide every minor dispute themselves. Make it easier for yourself by letting them share the burden with you.

Exodus 18:21–22

Just before Moses ascended Mount Sinai to receive the Ten Commandments, he learned a powerful lesson from his father-in-law.

What was the lesson that Moses learned? ______________________

If we do not seek help or advice from others, or share responsibilities, we all wear ourselves out.

Though we often feel an obligation to complete a task ourselves, sometimes situations require collaboration. Though Moses was the leader of the Israelites, he quickly learned that a true leader seeks advice and assistance from others.

The leader of your program has followed Jethro's advice in creating the tzadikim program at your school. How is this program similar to the text above?

Our religious school director could not take care of all student's and their learning needs without our help and the help of others.

How might you follow Jethro's advice working as a tzadik(ah)?

Whenever I am having difficulty working with my student, I should seek the advice of my learning consultant or educator.

Notes:

Participants are asked to list strategies that have not been working. This part of the lesson will reinforce the message that even if a strategy does not seem to work at first, it is important to try it again.

When Something Is Just Not Working

Now that you have spent time examining what works, take a look at the strategies that did not get stars. List them below:

Refer to Workbook page 194

Should you keep trying these strategies just because they are stated on your learning plan? The answer is yes and no. There is a process to follow before disregarding a strategy. Though you have powerful insight in your direct contact with your student, you must also consult with others who will help you make these important decisions. The process for reevaluating a student's learning plan is a simple one—you just have to remember the "TASC" at hand:

T ry the strategy again, even if it fails the first few times.
A sk your supervisor or teacher for help.
S hare the techniques that have been successful.
C ollaborate to find a new strategy.

Try again, **A**sk, **S**hare, **C**ollaborate. Through this task (TASC), you will find the most successful plan for your student.

Learning Needs of Students Often Change As They Mature

As your student is growing and maturing, his or her needs are changing as well. Some of the most successful strategies can break down overnight as students begin to see the world through more mature eyes.

Applying What You Learned

Justin (your student) is a third grader. Last year he worked with a *tzadik* using a behavior chart. The *tzadik* gave him stars throughout the day to help reinforce good behaviors. At the beginning of this year, you were instructed on the learning plan to use a behavior chart with Justin again. Justin liked his behavior chart at the beginning of the year, but now he keeps telling you that he does not need it. The more time you have spent with him, the more you realize that his behaviors are improving and you are able to help him participate in classroom activities using the other strategies you were taught during orientation. What should you do? Should you continue using the behavior chart with Justin?

Write down what you would do to cover each step of this "TASC":

T I would try to use the behavior chart again.

A I would ask my supervisor if we can stop using the chart.

S I would tell my supervisor all the other successful techniques we've used and explain that he is doing better on his own.

C We would decide if there were a better strategy to reinforce good behavior.

The facilitator should introduce the TASC method below and carefully ex- plain all four steps with examples.

Try the strategy again, even if it fails the first few times.

- If a student's learning plan advises you to create a behavior chart for the student and he tells you he doesn't like it, try using the chart again during the next ses- sion, but with stickers of his favorite cartoon character.

Ask your supervisor or teacher for help.

- If a student is given preferential seating at the front of the classroom but is distracting others in the classroom, ask your teacher or learning coordinator where a better seating location might be.

Share the techniques that have been successful.

- If you notice that writing the sound of the Hebrew letter on a sticky note at the top of her desk helps your student remember the sound she is learning, share this with your supervisor.

Collaborate to find a new strategy.

- If different preferential seating does not stop your student's disruptive behaviors, discuss this with the learning coordinator to help find a better strategy to help
- One review exercise is to erase the words on the whiteboard next to the acronym **TASC** and ask participants to explain all four steps in the process

Follow-up Question (after reading the introductory paragraph):

- "Can you think of an example of how a maturity change may alter a student's need? " (Speech may improve with age; behavior may improve as the student gets older and learns to feel embarrassed when he or she misbehaves.)

Refer to Workbook page 195

Notes:
The facilitator should lead a discussionabout behavior charts. Be sure to point out that behavior charts are not always the best method of reinforcement, but work well in many cases. As children mature, however, many of them outgrow this particular system or become embarrassed by it.

Discuss this case as a group. Are there certain ages when behavior charts no longer work? Is it the same for every child? Could you readapt the concept of a behavior chart into another system? How?

Ask: "Can you come up with any ways to modify a behavior chart so it becomes another kind of positive reward system for older students?" Some suggested answers:

(1) use intrinsic rewards (such as athumbs-up, a wink, or verbal praise), or

(2) if you notice a lot of good behaviors, give your student a surprise, etc.

Are there any strategies on your current learning plan that are no longer working for your student? If so, what are they?

1. ______
2. ______
3. ______

Next, the facilitator should have *tzadikim* look at their lists of strategies that are no longer working. Participants should read one unsuccessful strategy at a time out loud and attempt to explain why they think it is no longer working. If they cannot come up with a reason, others in the class should be given the opportunity to share their thoughts.

Why do you think these are no longer working?

______

• Ask participants to list any additional strategies that they have found to works on their own and then share them with the larger group. If a strategy is presented that is counter-productive (such as "I give my student a piece of candy for each word he reads in a sentence"), explain why another strategy may be better, always stressing how much you value the work of the *tzadikim*.

• Review the last question in the section that reminds *tzadikim* to speak to their supervisor each time they introduce a new strategy.

Have you found other strategies that have worked with your student? If yes, list them below. When you finish, share them with the group.

1. ______
2. ______
3. ______

Have you done anything to ensure that your supervisor or teacher knows about the strategies you listed above? If you haven't done anything yet, what should you now do, according to your "TASC" plan? ______

Review the last question in the section that reminds *tzadikim* to speak to their supervisor each time they introduce a new strategy.

______

Refer to Workbook page 196

Chevruta Study

Jewish tradition teaches that we learn best when we discuss an issue or a text with a partner. This is called "*chevruta* study." Work with a partner. Each pair should choose at least one scenario. With your partner, read over the student's information and the strategies, and then discuss if the strategy is working, other possible strategies, and where you would go to get assistance, if needed.

Every time Ms. Gold introduces a new activity, Ronny, your first-grade student, seems like he is lost in space. Ronny's learning plan suggests that you repeat directions to him. When the teacher gives directions, you try to do this, but he still seems to still be lost. This time, you decide to . . .

The learning plan for your second-grader, Leslie, suggests that you take Leslie for short walks as frequent breaks to help her re-focus. She loves going on walks with you; however, you find that her time out of the classroom seems to actually cause her to have more problems reorienting and focusing on the activity at hand once you get back in the classroom. Upon reentering the classroom this time, you . . .

Michael, your third-grade student, tells you that he is embarrassed that you always sit right next to him. He asks if you can sit in the back of the classroom instead. You're not sure if you will be able to carry out your assigned strategies if you are so far away, but you also want to respect his feelings. So you . . .

Allison seems to be falling significantly behind in Hebrew class. You are following all the suggestions on her learning plan, but she is not learning any of the Hebrew letters and you are growing concerned. Her second-grade year is now more than half over. As you are working today, you decide to . . .

Dylan is the only pre-K student in the class who can't sit still. His learning plan states that when Dylan is fidgety, he should be allowed to move around. Mrs. Wasser has asked you to try to keep him in his seat. Nothing you try seems to work. At this point, you . . .

After *chevruta* study, answer the following questions as a group.

- Was the original strategy fully implemented?
- Was it successful?
- If not, why did the strategy fail?
- Should the *tzadik(ah)* try it again?
- How might he or she try it in a different way?
- What other strategies may work better in this situation?

. . . simplify the directions or break them into smaller parts, write them down so he can see them, add gestures and other visuals and add eye contact, etc.

. . . remind her what the class was working on just before you took the walk, give her an assignment when she walks into the classroom, walk with her to her chair and prepare all the materials she will need to continue working (such as her workbook and pencil), etc.

. . . sit a row behind him instead of next to him; don't sit, but rather walk around the classroom, always staying close by, etc.

. . . make five flashcards of the first five letters and take her outside to play memory games with them, bring some moldable dough and pipe cleaners and help her form letters on her desk, have her trace one letter at a time with her finger, etc.

. . . ask Mrs. Wasser if you can speak to her privately for a minute and suggest that Dylan's desk could be placed at the back of the class- room so that he can get up when he needs to, be allowed to stand all the time, or be allowed to run errands and take breaks more often, etc.

Notes:

- Participants are divided into pairs and one scenario is distributed to each pair. If there are more than five pairs, the same scenario can be given to more than one pair. If there are fewer than five pairs, the instructor should choose which scenarios to use.
- Participant pairs should spend five min- utes discussing their scenarios.
- When the group comes back together, have each pair present their findings. The fol- lowing questions should be used as a guide.
- Remember that the goal of this section is to remind tzadikim to always seek addi tional help before abandoning a strategy or adding new strategies. Therefore, all groups should ack nowledge that they would seek the help of the learning consultant or educator.

Workshop IV: Facilitating the Curriculum

The final workshop session should be conducted during the last few weeks of school. As noted earlier, the final workshop has two functions: (1) to facilitate personal reflection for the *tzadikim* and (2) to assist the learning consultant and strengthen the program. Even with the best assistants and strategies in place, some students may only make minimal progress over the course of the year. In these cases, the learning consultant should reassure *tzadikim* that their performance is good, but that the intensity of the student's special need has hindered that student's overall success. In addition, this information should be provided to future *tzadikim* so that they will have proper expectations for the year. If the student's lack of progress is a product of a *tzadik(ah)'s* poor performance, thought should be given to setting up the best match for the student with the special need for the next year. Additionally, the learning consultant should clearly communicate to the *tzadikim* their strengths and weaknesses in this role, so that they will be aware of them in future endeavors and teaching opportunities.

In larger schools with a greater number of *tzadikim*, the learning consultant may ask the educator to attend this session so that more time can be devoted to each participant. After they evaluate the growth of the *tzadikim* through the questionnaire, the facilitators may choose to have one-on-one meetings with each participant, rather than having the *tzadikim* work with their peers (as suggested in the *tzadikim* guide). During these one-on-one meetings, the *tzadik* or *tzadikah* and the educator should read over the student's entire learning plan, making notes, additions, and deletions on the document as they work. As part of the program, *tzadikim* rank the strategies from most effective to least effective. The learning consultant should use this information to update the learning plan for the next school year. If your congregation does not yet have formal learning plans, this workshop will be an opportunity for the learning consultant to take detailed notes on effective strategies (from whatever document is being used) that can be incorporated into the creation of a learning plan.

This session also helps *tzadikim* gain a clear understanding of all the ways the experience may have made an impact on and enriched their personal lives. The self-evaluation is intended to highlight some of the leadership traits they see in themselves. It is up to the educator or the learning consultant to highlight the *tzadikim's* leadership in a spiritual context. This can be accomplished by completing a one-page evaluation of each *tzadik(ah)* (Appendix I). The evaluation should include key Jewish concepts in the description of their leadership skills, such as "being a partner with God," "modeling *kavod ha'briut* (preserving another human's dignity)," "enabling others to do mitzvot," etc. In addition to public recognition at the end of the year, a positive evaluation will go a long way toward keeping this teenager on a Jewish leadership track in the future.

Notes

Refer to Workbook page 197

WORKSHOP IV

Self-Study Exercises

(to be completed prior to attending Workshop IV)

The goal of the *tzadikim* program is not only to help students with learning differences succeed in religious school, but also to help create the next generation of Jewish educational leaders. The skills you have developed during the school year are skills that cannot be acquired in even the highest-level college courses. Your hands-on experience over this past year will help you succeed in high school and beyond.

The Mishnah teaches that* mitzvah goreret mitzvah *or "one mitzvah leads to another"* (Pirkei Avot 4:2)*. What do you think this rabbinic verse means and how might it be related to your work during the school year? ______

This verse means that when we model positive acts, it leads to others performing positive acts. When we work with students who need assistance and guidance, other people see the value in helping others and treating each person as important, no matter what his or her needs.

Ask participants to share some of their answers to the three opinion-based questions. Acknowledge all answers in a positive way and repeat back some of the key phrases participants use. (Use active listening here. For example, if a student says, "I have learned to slow down and become a more patient person because it always took my student a long time to complete each page in his workbook," an appropriate response would be, "It sounds like you have learned a lot about being patient.")

When a student practices a skill regularly, not only does he or she become better at it, but it slowly becomes a natural and comfortable part of his or her approach to learning. The more you practice the skills you have learned as a *tzadik(ah)*, the more they will become part of your regular teaching style. Hopefully, your experience this year will lead you to a lifetime of positive teaching and modeling skills, as well as a desire to help and advocate for others.

In addition, in the time that you and your student have spent together you should have forged a mutually beneficial relationship. Just as your student has grown from your help, you have also grown in many ways.

How have you seen your student grow (physically, intellectually, or emotionally) since the beginning of the year? ______________________

____

____

____

Refer to Workbook page 198

How do you feel that you have grown (physically, intellectually, or emotionally)? ______

______

______

______

______

______

______

To prepare for the upcoming session, briefly describe two or three memorable (both positive and negative) episodes or experiences with your student. Do not worry about writing in complete sentences.

______

______

______

______

______

______

______

______

______

______

The second question (How do you feel that you have grown . . . ?) may be more difficult for middle and high school students to answer, as they may struggle to see self-growth and verbalize it. Be prepared to share prewritten statements from Appendix I if participants struggle when sharing their answers

Prepare:

- Bring copies of the Learning Plan Evaluations (with foil stars) created in Workshop III.
- The learning consultant or educator should review any written notes about tzadikim performance during the year before filling out the *Tzadik(ah)* Evaluation (Appendix I). Although it is suggested to just write down key phrases to share orally with *tzadikim*, you may choose to give *tzadikim* a copy of the document.
- Fill out one *Tzadik(ah)* Evaluation (Appendix I) for each student. The last question may be used when reviewing the self-evaluation at the beginning of the session. To answer this, think of at least one or two ways that you think each of the *tzadikim* has grown throughout the year (and, if you have noticed any particular situations with their students where you have witnessed them learning something, or "aha" moments). These do not have to be profound statements for participants who may have struggled throughout the year. For instance, statements like, "Jon has learned the importance of handicap accessibility in schools and synagogues," or "Lisa has learned to understand the importance of role-modeling positive treatment of others."
- Make notes or write out a script for your final words to the group. These will be your own words of inspiration to the group before you end the session.
- This workshop can be run in a variety of different ways, depending on the number of tzadikim and the number of facilitators. Although suggestions are given here, think carefully about your program needs and the success of previous workshops before planning the final session.

Notes:

- Before giving *tzadikim* time to begin working on their questionnaires, set the context of the importance of these evaluations. Explain that their observations will play a major role in creating a better plan for their student next year and encourage them to give the most concrete exampl esthey can. If applicable, let them know that you will be discussing their answers with them in one-on-one private conversations after they complete the questionnaires.
- Pass out Learning Plan Evaluations (the Learning Plan Evaluation Exercise from Workshop III) to *tzadikim* and give them a minute or two to review their answers.
- Provide at least fifteen minutes for *tzadikim* to complete the questionnaires. Tell them not to get hung up on any answers and that their first thought is probably the best answer.
- You may choose whether to begin one-on-one meetings immediately after they have completed the student growth questionnaire or wait until they have completed their own growth questionnaires.
- Provide about ten minutes for *tzadikim* to complete the Recognizing Your Growth as a Special Needs Facilitator questionnaire.
- During one-on-one meetings, quickly glance over their student questionnaires, looking for inconsistencies (sections where the numbers jump in one or more areas) to discuss. Also, ask participants to read their leadership description paragraphs to you.

WORKSHOP IV

Planning for the Next School Year and Self-evaluation

Objectives: By the end of this workshop, you will:

- Evaluate your student's growth over the current year.
- Provide input for a learning plan for the next school year.
- Recognize your growth as a special needs facilitator.
- Understand how your role as a *tzadik(ah)* relates to your Jewish spiritual growth.

As the end of the school year is approaching, this workshop will give you the opportunity to assist in planning for your student for the upcoming school year, as well as to evaluate your own growth during this past school year. In Workshop III, you were given the task of reevaluating your student's needs. Now take that a step further. The following questionnaire is designed to assist you in evaluating your student holistically from the start to the end of this school year.

Evaluating Your Student's Growth

The purpose of this questionnaire is to evaluate your student's growth in the following three areas since the beginning of this school year:

- Behavior
- Learning
- Social/Emotional Development

Use the following five-point scale to answer the questions:

5 – Excellent
4 – Above Average
3 – Average
2 – Below Average
1 – Poor

Refer to Workbook page 200

Circle a 1, 2, 3, 4, or 5 following each question.

SECTION 1: BEHAVIOR

1. At the very beginning of the school year, how would you rate your student's general classroom behavior when under your direct supervision?

   1 2 3 4 5

2. By the middle of the school year, how would you rate your student's general classroom behavior when under your direct supervision?

   1 2 3 4 5

3. How would you now rate your student's general classroom behavior when under your direct supervision?

   1 2 3 4 5

4. At the very beginning of the school year, how would you rate your student's ability to focus and pay attention when under your direct supervision?

   1 2 3 4 5

5. By the middle of the school year, how would you rate your student's ability to focus and pay attention when under your direct supervision?

   1 2 3 4 5

6. How would you now rate your student's general classroom ability to focus and pay attention when under your direct supervision?

   1 2 3 4 5

Did your student's general classroom behavior improve since the beginning of the year? Why or why not? ______________________________

____

____

____

Refer to Workbook page 201

Did your student's ability to focus and pay attention improve since the beginning of the year? Why or why not? ______________________________

____

____

____

____

SECTION 2: LEARNING

1. At the very beginning of the school year, how would you rate your student's general ability to grasp new concepts when under your direct supervision?

   1 2 3 4 5

2. By the middle of the school year, how would you rate your student's general ability to grasp new concepts when under your direct supervision?

   1 2 3 4 5

3. How would you now rate your student's general ability to grasp new concepts when under your direct supervision?

   1 2 3 4 5

4. At the very beginning of the school year, how would you rate your student's overall retention level of the material presented by his or her teacher(s)?

   1 2 3 4 5

5. By the middle of the school year, how would you rate your student's overall retention level of the material presented by his or her teacher(s)?

   1 2 3 4 5

6. How would you now rate your student's overall retention level of the material presented by his or her teacher(s)?

   1 2 3 4 5

Refer to Workbook page 202

Did your student's general ability to grasp new concepts improve since the beginning of the year? Why or why not? ______________________

____

____

____

____

Did your student's overall retention of the material presented by his or her teacher(s) improve since the beginning of the year? Why or why not? ______________________

____

____

____

____

SECTION 3: SOCIAL/EMOTIONAL DEVELOPMENT

1. At the very beginning of the school year, how would you rate your student's overall maturity?

   1 2 3 4 5

2. By the middle of the school year, how would you rate your student's overall maturity?

   1 2 3 4 5

3. How would you now rate your student's overall maturity?

   1 2 3 4 5

4. At the very beginning of the school year, how would you rate your student's ability to make friends and socialize with the other students?

   1 2 3 4 5

5. By the middle of the school year, how would you rate your student's ability to make friends and socialize with the other students?

   1 2 3 4 5

6. How would you now rate your student's ability to make friends and socialize with the other students?

   1 2 3 4 5

Did your student's overall maturity improve since the beginning of the year? Why or why not? ______________________________

____

____

____

____

Did your student's ability to make friends and socialize with the other students improve since the beginning of the year? Why or why not?

____

____

____

____

____

You have probably learned many things from the questionnaire. Likely, your confidence and ability to anticipate your student's needs, and monitor and provide appropriate interventions, have helped your student to show improvement in at least one of the three areas on which you just reflected. It is also likely that your student has grown and matured through the year and is perhaps requiring fewer interventions and demonstrating more frequent success in the classroom. Yet there is also a possibility that due to circumstances beyond your control and/or a complex developmental or learning disability, your student has made no notable improvements in any of these three areas. If this is the case, it is important to reflect on what your interventions have accomplished. Would your student be able to participate in a regular classroom without you present? Has your student benefited from being in a Jewish environment and having positive Jewish experiences as a direct result of your presence? The answer to both of these questions is yes.

Refer to Workbook page 204

Work with a partner and share the results of your student evaluation.

Finalizing the Learning Plan

In Workshop III, you reevaluated your student's learning plan by placing foil stars next to the items you would continue to utilize as well as noting which interventions were no longer necessary. You also noted additional interventions that you found effective. As you approach the end of the year, and with the completion of the evaluation questionnaire, revisit your student's learning plan one more time.

Review your notes from Workshop III, assess your student's most recent progress, and utilize this knowledge to "finalize" what you think your student's learning plan should look like for the next school year (the actual learning plan will be determined by the learning consultant, with input from parents, teachers, and especially the *tzadik* or *tzadikah*). Use a pen or pencil to cross out any interventions you find do not work anymore and rank those that are effective in order of importance (i.e., place a number 1 next to the most effective strategy, a number 2 next the second most effective strategy, and so on). If you use strategies not currently listed on the learning plan, write them down on the bottom or the back of the page. Take ten minutes to complete this exercise individually then turn in your finalized version to your supervisor for review.

Recognizing Your Growth as a Special Needs Facilitator

As you have probably discovered this year, everyone learns differently. Some people are oral learners and others are visual learners. Some people learn by doing and others like to learn from a book. But as a special needs facilitator, you have learned a great deal by seeing the world through another person's eyes. And as you have gained an awareness of the way students learn, you have probably discovered that we all have learning differences. This means that you have become a much more empathetic young adult.

But empathy is not the only skill you have gained through this program. Using the same five-point system you used to evaluate your student's growth throughout the school year, assess how you have grown this year. You will be evaluating your growth over the year in the following four areas:

- Patience
- Leadership
- Empathy
- Being a Role Model

As a reminder, use the following five-point scale to answer the questions:

5 – Excellent
4 – Above Average
3 – Average
2 – Below Average
1 – Poor

Circle a 1, 2, 3, 4, or 5 following each question.

SECTION 1: PATIENCE

1. At the very beginning of the school year, how would you rate your overall patience when working with your student?

   1 2 3 4 5

2. By the middle of the school year, how would you rate your overall patience when working with your student?

   1 2 3 4 5

3. How would you now rate your overall patience when working with your student?

   1 2 3 4 5

SECTION 2: LEADERSHIP

1. At the very beginning of the school year, how would you rate your overall leadership skills?

   1 2 3 4 5

2. By the middle of the school year, how would you rate your overall leadership skills?

   1 2 3 4 5

3. How would you now rate your overall leadership skills?

   1 2 3 4 5

Refer to Workbook page 206

SECTION 3: EMPATHY

1. At the very beginning of the school year, how would you rate your overall empathy for those with learning differences?

   1 2 3 4 5

2. By the middle of the school year, how would you rate your overall empathy for those with learning differences?

   1 2 3 4 5

3. How would you now rate your overall empathy for those with learning differences?

   1 2 3 4 5

SECTION 4: BEING A ROLE MODEL

1. How would you rate yourself as a role model at the very beginning of the school year?

   1 2 3 4 5

2. How would you rate yourself as a role model in the middle of the school year?

   1 2 3 4 5

3. How would you now rate yourself as a role model?

   1 2 3 4 5

Refer to Workbook page 207

Read the following adjectives. Place a check next to each of the adjectives that describe you as a leader.

___ empathetic	___ caring	___ intuitive	___ strong
___ fair	___ religious	___ intelligent	___ observant
___ focused	___ organized	___ authoritative	___ charismatic
___ compassionate	___ admirable	___ modest	___ polished
___ thoughtful	___ talented	___ generous	___ passionate
___ dynamic	___ honest	___ resourceful	___ loyal
___ patriotic	___ gregarious	___ mindful	___ cautious
___ sincere	___ gracious	___ praiseworthy	___ trustworthy
___ ethical	___ commendable	___ humble	___ daring

Refer to Workbook page 208

When you apply to college and go on job interviews, you are often asked to describe your leadership skills. For most people, this is not an easy task. However, by evaluating your growth as a *tzadik(ah)*, you have identified some of your leadership skills.

Using the four evaluation sections above, in addition to the list of adjectives, write a paragraph describing your leadership skills as a special needs facilitator. Present yourself as if you were applying for a job.

___

___

___

___

___

___

___

Understanding How Your Role as a Tzadik(ah) Relates to Your Jewish Spiritual Growth

> "Man was given a share in His wisdom and is called to responsible living and to be a partner of God in the redemption of the world."
>
> —Abraham Joshua Heschel (*God in Search of Man*, p. 66)

Abraham Joshua Heschel, one of the greatest Jewish thinkers of the twentieth century, often spoke about our role as God's partners in bettering the world. God gives a special talent to every living creature. Some of us excel in sports, some in academics, some in art. Others have the gift of humor or are good at problem solving. Your gift of compassion and dedication to helping others makes you God's partner in perfecting the world. Whether you are a regular synagogue attendee or not, you possess a divine spark within you that helps bring our world one step closer to perfection. Working with students with special needs makes you a very holy and spiritual person, whether you knew it or not!
Complete these sentences.

Refer to Workbook page 209

When I work with my student, I feel

When I perform this mitzvah, I feel a connection with God because

After studying to be a tzadik(ah) *this year, I have learned that Judaism teaches*

Conclusion

Lech L'cha: Be a Change Agent for the Future of Jewish Education

The journey before you is a big one, but it is a sacred one. You will be opening a Jewish path for those for whom such a path may have been closed before. In a world where these families have to fight for their children, you and your faculty can take their hand and lead them spiritually. But, before you begin your journey, you should know that there will be many pitfalls along the way. With each success, there are challenges; and sometimes, as much as you give and you try, a family who is struggling may even blame you for their failures. When we were struggling to find a solution for one family, a gifted pediatrician and lay leader told us, "I know it is difficult when they blame us for trying to help them. But each time they take it out on you, remember this: If they don't blame you, they are going to blame themselves. We will never know what it is like to be in their situation. Just be happy you can be there to share their burden."

With every child you assist, you also help improve a family's life. Aside from the pain you may feel when helping challenging families, you will also derive the greatest pleasure from seeing the success of your labor. A child with autism becoming bar mitzvah, a young girl with mitochondrial disease singing in a school performance, a community of children embracing a classmate in a wheelchair—these are just some of the most memorable images that remind us why we take an additional step to think outside the box for a child's education. When we see the way a child with special needs looks up to a teenage *tzadik* or *tzadikah*, we are confident that this is what is meant by being partners with God. Now it is your turn to make a change in the life of a child, a family, and the future of Judaism.

The following story about a water carrier, by an anonymous writer, carries a message calling us to action: Once there was a water carrier who carried two vessels hanging from two sides of a pole on his shoulders. Each day he would leave the king's palace and carry the vessels across a valley and up a hill until he reached a spring, where he would dip the vessels in the water and fill them up for his return. The vessel that hung on his right was a perfectly shaped clay pot, while the one on the left was old and chipped, with a crack on the side of it. The perfect pot was so proud of its ability to assist the water carrier in his duties, but the cracked pot was quite ashamed of its imperfections. Every time that water carrier filled the pots, the vessel on his left would slowly leak water the whole way back to the palace, making it more and more difficult for the water carrier to trudge up the hill, as the pots were out of balance on his shoulders.

One day, as he made his way across the valley, he heard the vessel on the left weeping. As he approached the water, he asked the pot why it was crying. It answered, "My master, I am so ashamed of my imperfection. I want to apologize for all the extra work I have caused you because of my flaw, making your job of carrying water even more difficult."

The water carrier, who was a compassionate soul, answered the cracked pot and said, "My dear friend. Do not be ashamed. Today, after I fill you with water and we walk back to the palace, I want you to look down along the way as we make our journey."

The flawed pot shed a final tear and agreed to observe the path during their return. As they began to walk, he noticed that on his side of the path there were beautiful flowers leading up the hill and across the valley—the entire way from the spring to the palace. The pot said to the water carrier, "I have never noticed all these beautiful flowers."

The water carrier replied, "Yes, my friend, they are very beautiful. I want you to notice that they are only on this side of the path, and not on the other. You see, years ago, when I first noticed your imperfection, I decided to take advantage of it. I began planting seeds as we walked back from the spring. Every day as we have walked down this path, you have given life to those seeds by dripping water from the crack in your side. What you have always thought of as a flaw, in actuality has brought beauty to this world."

The water carrier's work helping the vessel overcome its imperfection did not come overnight. It was a slow process that involved much thought and preparation; yet, it made a permanent impact on the vessel's future. In the Jewish educational world, we have so many vessels waiting to be touched by our creativity, insight, and compassion. As you begin your journey now across the meadow and over the hill toward creating an inclusive synagogue community, may the vessels that you lift up bring forth gardens of hope for all families who enter your congregation and your community. *Lech l'cha* (Go forth) on your journey toward change!

Appendicies

Appendix A

Additional Suggested Resources on Special Needs

Biel, Lindsey, and Nancy K. Peske. *Raising a Sensory Smart Child: The Definitive Handbook for Helping Your Child with Sensory Processing Issues*, updated and rev. ed. New York: Penguin Books, 2009. Print.

Boring, Melinda L. *Heads Up Helping! Teaching Tips and Techniques for Working with ADD, ADHD, and Other Children with Challenges.* Victoria, B.C., Canada: Trafford, 2002. Print.

Conners, Susan. *The Tourette Syndrome & OCD Checklist: A Practical Reference for Parents and Teachers.* San Francisco: Jossey-Bass, 2011. Print.

Dacey, John S., and Lisa B. Fiore. *Your Anxious Child: How Parents and Teachers Can Relieve Anxiety in Children.* San Francisco: Jossey-Bass, 2000. Print.

Gillingham, Gail. *Autism, Handle with Care! Understanding and Managing Behavior of Children and Adults with Autism.* Arlington, Tex.: Future Education, 1995. Print.

Greydanus, Donald E., Dilip R. Patel, and Helen D. Pratt. *Developmental Disabilities.* Philadelphia: Saunders, 2009. Print.

Hallowell, Edward M. *When You Worry about the Child You Love: Emotional and Learning Problems in Children.* New York: Simon & Schuster, 1996. Print.

Hallowell, Edward M., and John J. Ratey. *Driven to Distraction: Recognizing and Coping with Attention Deficit Disorder from Childhood through Adulthood.* New York: Simon & Schuster, 1995. Print.

Powers, Michael D. *Children with Autism: A Parent's Guide*, 2nd ed. Bethesda, Md.: Woodbine House, 2000. Print.

Shaywitz, Sally. *Overcoming Dyslexia.* New York: Alfred A. Knopf, 2003. Print.

Silver, Larry B. *The Misunderstood Child: Understanding and Coping with Your Child's*

Learning Disabilities, 3rd ed. New York: Times Books, 1998. Print.

Smith, Karen A., and Karen R. Gouze. *The Sensory-Sensitive Child: Practical Solutions for Out-of-Bounds Behavior*. New York: HarperResource, 2004. Print.

Vail, Priscilla L. *Smart Kids with School Problems: Things to Know and Ways to Help*. New York: Dutton, 1987. Print.

——. *Emotion: The On/Off Switch for Learning*. Rosemont, N.J.: Modern Learning Press, 1994. Print.

Webb, James T. *A Parent's Guide to Gifted Children*. Scottsdale, Ariz.: Great Potential Press, 2007. Print.

Appendix B

Suggested Opening Stories for Workshops and Meetings

Welcome to Holland

by Emily Perl Kingsley

I am often asked to describe the experience of raising a child with disability—to try to help people who have not shared that unique experience to understand it, to imagine how it would feel. It's like this . . .

When you're going to have a baby, it's like planning a fabulous vacation trip—to Italy. You buy a bunch of guidebooks and make your wonderful plans. The Coliseum. The Michelangelo *David*. The gondolas in Venice. You may learn some handy phrases in Italian. It's all very exciting.

After months of eager anticipation, the day finally arrives. You pack your bags and off you go. Several hours later, the plane lands. The stewardess comes in and says, "Welcome to Holland."

"Holland?!?" you say. "What do you mean Holland?? I signed up for Italy! I'm supposed to be in Italy. All my life I've dreamed of going to Italy."

But there's been a change in the flight plan. They've landed in Holland and there you must stay.

The important thing is that they haven't taken you to a horrible, disgusting, filthy place, full of pestilence, famine, and disease. It's just a different place.

So you must go out and buy new guidebooks. And you must learn a whole new language. And you will meet a whole new group of people you would never have met.

It's just a different place. It's slower-paced than Italy, less flashy than Italy. But after you've been there for a while and you catch your breath, you look around . . . and you begin to notice that Holland has windmills . . . and Holland has tulips. Holland even has Rembrandts.

But everyone you know is busy coming and going from Italy . . . and they're all bragging about what a wonderful time they had there. And for the rest of your life, you will say, "Yes, that's where I was supposed to go. That's what I had planned."

And the pain of that will never, ever, ever, ever go away . . . because the loss of that dream is a very, very significant loss.

But . . . if you spend your life mourning the fact that you didn't get to Italy, you may never be free to enjoy the very special, the very lovely things . . . about Holland.

Benjamin

by Dori Courtney

Even before school started, I knew all about my incoming first-graders. Their kindergarten teachers spoke of the students in glowing terms, except for one. Benjamin, they said, wasn't like other children; he didn't like stories, he couldn't sit still and he didn't have respect for other people's property. He was like a wild animal, eating out of the garbage and running amok. They sympathetically wished me luck.

On the first day of school, I talked with the children about the routines and procedures of first grade. Benjamin, as advertised, had a hard time sitting at group time, staying in his seat or following directions.

After story time, I asked if anyone felt like sharing his or hers fears or hopes for the new school year. I got the ball rolling by telling them that I couldn't sleep the night before because I had butterflies in my stomach. The children shared their thoughts and we decided to draw pictures of what we wanted to happen during first grade. I figured the pictures would make a good class book and remind us of our goals for the year.

Most children drew themselves playing with friends eating in the cafeteria or reading a book. I cautiously approached Benjamin, who had been alternately drawing with and nibbling on his crayons. We'd only been in school about two hours, and his area already looked like a disaster.

"Benjamin, you used beautiful colors," I said, helping him pick up hi scattered crayons. "Tell me about your drawing." It looks like a jumble of scribbles, lines and dots.

"It's you'n me," he said, his eyes on his work. "See? I'm over here with my net, and there's butterflies living in your stomach."

I laughed, taken by surprise.

"So there are?" I said, striving for a serious expression. "I like your picture, but I was hoping you'd draw what you want to happen this year."

"I did," was all he'd say.

"He never does what he's supposed to." Laurie informed me. Soon other children began telling me how awful Benjamin had been the previous year. It was clear to me that Benjamin carried major baggage from kindergarten, and he'd need all of our help to clear it away.

"Everything is different in first grade," I said, giving Benjamin a conspiratorial wink.

I showed Benjamin's picture to his kindergarten teacher when she asked if I survived my first day. She smiled and said, "Well, it's better than a picture he drew last year. I felt so bad—he drew our school on fire and told me that's how I felt about him. I truly wish you better luck with that child than I had."

Her words pierced my heart. It became my mission to help Benjamin relate to ther children, feel safe and secure in school, and learn to read and write.

When I called to discuss Ben's difficulties, his stepmom assured me he was stubborn, not stupid. She made him sit for two hours at home so he'd know how to sit at school.

I stopped calling when she suggested, "just hit him, he'll settle down." I knew she was receiving parenting classes in her home, and I prayed that Benjamin would benefit from them one day.

In time, most kids began to accept Benjamin, but no one beside me called him "friend." He learned some social skills, but no matter what accommodations, incentives, or one-on-one support I offered, Benjamin wasn't able to concentrate on learning. I sent him to second grade, sure he'd end of friendless and in special education classes. I felt like I failed hijm.

During his second-grade year, Benjamin visted me everyday before school. He'd come in munching on a muffin from the school cafeteria, crumbs flying everywhere and say, "Good morning, Mrs. Courtney. Have a good day." I'd give him a hug and send him on his way with whatever inspirational words of wisdom I had handy.

At the whole-school assembly on the first day of his third-grade year, Benjamin told me he was going to be a good boy. I told him he'd always been a good boy.

"No," he said, as if I was a little slow. "I'm goin' to listen 'cause I wanna learn." I told him I thought that was a good plan. And incredibly, Benjamin did learn to read that year. He carried around a notebook and wrote constantly—wonderful, imaginative stories.

Benjamin's in fourth grade now and doesn't visit me anymore. I asked him why and he said simply, "I'm in fourth grade." I was saddened by his cavalier attitude but had to admit that he was entitled to make his own decisions.

When asked to write letters of encouragement to fourth-graders taking the in-depth standardized tests required by our state, I chose Benjamin. I told him I was proud of how hard he was working in school and that he'd do well on the test if he used the strategies he'd been taught. I concluded by saying I didn't know what had caused him to take school seriously, but I was really glad he had.

The next day, Benjamin came into my room, munching on a cinnamon roll, crumbs trailing behind him, and handed me a large envelope. I said, "Good morning, Benjamin. Read your test carefully, okay? I know you'll do your best." He just smiled and gave me a thumbs-up.

Later that morning, while my students were at art, I looked at the envelope. Benjamin had written a note of the outside. It said:

Dear Mrs. Courtney,

The answer is in here. Please be careful with it. I'll pick it up at the end of the day.

Love, Benjamin

The envelope held a picture of his first-grade class, a letter from his Sunday school teacher asking where he'd been and hoping he'd return soon, three copies of newspapers articles he'd appeared in during first grade, a certificate from his brother's teacher commending him for helping her clean her room and earning himself a yearbook, a beautifully drawn picture of Benjamin and his stepmom, several notes from me, and a certificate for reading to my class. Everything was in pristine condition. I stood staring at the contents of the envelope trying to decide how the mementos added up to success in school as his note indicated.

Then it struck me, the items came from people in his life who cared about him. I had a good cry that day, and I don't think I'll worry about students in the same way again. No, I hadn't taught Benjamin to read as I'd had hoped. But, somehow, I had helped prepare him for learning. The envelope told me Benjamin knew that.

Appendix C

Sample Student Referral Form for Teachers

(Adapted with permission from Ellen Maiseloff, Jewish Federation of Metropolitan Detroit)

Student Name: ______________________________ Date: ____________________

Teacher Completing this Form: __________________ Signature: ____________________

Observable Classroom Behavior	Most of the time	Some of the time
Easily distracted		
Withdrawn		
Talks out of turn		
Responds to questions inappropriately		
Unable to sit still		
Impulsive		
Unable to pay attention		
Has difficulty getting along with peers		
Comes to class without books/supplies		
Works better alone		
Works better in groups		
Unreliable short-term memory (same day)		
Does not participate in class discussions		
Disorganized papers or desk		

Additional comments:

Academic Concerns	Most of the time	Some of the time
Reverses letters		
Omits letters		
Confuses similar letters		
Has difficulty deciphering a crowded page		
Unable to copy from whiteboard correctly		
Holds books close to eyes		
Has difficulty forming letters		
Has difficulty following oral directions		
Has difficulty learning sounds or reproducing sounds of letters		
Misunderstands what is said		
Needs directions repeated frequently		
Has difficulty reading aloud		
Seems not to understand or follow written instruction		

Additional Comments:

Appendix D

Suggested Outline for Staff Training

(This outline may be adapted to meet your specific time requirements.)

Materials:

- Mirrors
- Handouts
- Highlighters

Part 1: (55–60 minutes)

I. Icebreaker (5 minutes)

II. Introduction: Story and a Hebrew Text (5–10 minutes)
   A. "Welcome to Holland" or "Benjamin"
   B. Choose a text from page 160 of the *tzadikim* guide, the Rabbi Peraida story from page 161, or your own

III. Learning Differences 101: Identifying the Terminology (10 minutes)
   A. Pages 7–10 of the *tzadikim* guide

IV. Understanding Learning Differences by Practice (15 minutes)
   A. Dysgraphia/Visual Motor Perceptual Deficit
      1. Page 7 of the *tzadikim* guide
   B. Dyslexia/Visual Processing Deficit
      1. Page 7 of the *tzadikim* guide
   C. Auditory Processing
      1. Page 7 of the *tzadikim* guide

V. Basic Classroom Management Strategies for Students with Attention or Processing Delays (15 minutes)
   A. Pages 163–164 of the *tzadikim* guide

VI. Questions and Answers (5 minutes)

Break (20 minutes)

Part 2: (40 minutes)

I. Text Study (5 minutes)

II. Adapting Teaching Methods to Meet the Needs of Students with Reading-based Learning Differences (25 minutes)

A. Basic Strategies for Teaching Hebrew
   1. Page 164 of the *tzadikim* guide
B. Reading as a Dyslexic Student with/without Strategies
   1. Page 164 of the *tzadikim* guide
C. Adapting Your Text
   1. Hand out a copy of *V'ahavta* and have participants highlight it

IX. Questions (10 minutes)

Appendix E

Example of Clear and Positive Classroom Rules

Ms. Cohen's Ten Classroom Commandments

1. Raise your hand before speaking.
2. Show respect to each other.
3. Leave food and drinks at home.
4. Listen when the teacher is speaking.
5. Walk quietly in the hallways.
6. Sit quietly when someone else is speaking.
7. Always wait your turn.
8. Use your finger to follow along when reading.
9. Ask permission to leave the classroom.
10. Always do your best work.

Remember: Rules should always tell students what they *should* be doing . . . written in the positive.

Appendix F

Examples of Specific Classroom Modifications for Inclusive Programs

- Highlighting techniques for Hebrew reading
- Incentive charts and positive reward systems[1]
- Positive classroom rules, placed in a prominent spot
- Preferential seating
- Close attention to classroom setup
- Limited classroom distractions (such as too many wordy posters and signs around the room)
- Strategic placement of *madrichim* and *tzadikim*
- Accessible quiet spaces for one-on-one work with students or private work (which can be called a "concentration station")
- Enlarged print for children with dyslexia or visual deficits
- Using a finger, a pencil, or a *yad* to point to the text (all students in the classroom should be required to follow along whenever reading with these)
- Use of multisensory tools to teach phonics (forming bendable wax sticks or colored molding dough into the shape of the Hebrew letter for tactile feedback; tracing letters through shaving cream on a flat surface)
- Use of handheld manipulatives (multicolored rubber porcupine balls, stress balls, etc.)
- Personal FM amplification systems for children who are hard of hearing or those who have central auditory processing dis-

1 As noted earlier, there are new movements trending away from the use of extrinsic rewards; however, charts and stickers may be effective for many children.

orders (the teacher wears a microphone that amplifies his or her voice onto a small receiver located on the student's desk)

- Seat cushions for children with sensory processing disorders (special cushions, which are typically recommended for children by an occupational therapist, may provide additional tactile and sensory input to help these children sit in their seat and pay better attention to the teacher)
- Basic positive teaching strategies (as presented in Workshop I, Part 3 of the ***tzadikim*** guide)

Appendix G

Sample Learning Plan for Haim Rosen Academic Year 2011–2012

Information for the Teacher

Haim has been diagnosed with mild dyslexia, a learning difference in the area of reading. Haim becomes very embarrassed reading out loud, due to his delays in reading. Haim also has ADHD (attention-deficit/hyperactivity disorder); however, he takes daily medication to manage this. Due to poor auditory processing skills, listening proves challenging for him.

Suggestions for the Teacher to Be Implemented in the Classroom

1. The learning consultant or *tzadik* will take portions of his text and provide visual cues for syllable divisions (using alternating colors to show where the divisions occur).
2. Haim should not be asked to read out loud in class unless he volunteers to do so.
3. If Haim is reading one-on-one with the teacher, or if he is reading out loud to the class, try to use color-coded portions of the text to help Haim.
4. Be sure that Haim always uses his finger to point to the syllable/word he is reading.
5. Keep directions short and simple, and speak slowly. Repeat directions as needed. Use gestures when providing directions.
6. Provide preferential seating for Haim.
7. Give breaks often. If Haim seems to be having problems focusing, allow him to take a break. Having him run an errand for the teacher is a good way to accomplish this. Try to keep all the students moving.
8. Use a positive reinforcement behavior management system for the entire class (charts, displays, or secret systems). Establish and enforce rules with the input of the students, if possible. The fewer rules, the better. Al-

ways state rules in the positive and be sure to post expectations in the classroom.

9. If hyperactivity is an issue, simply ignore Haim if he is moving around or squirming in his seat.
10. Comment on Haim's positive behaviors as much as possible. Use nonverbal cues to stop inappropriate behaviors.
11. The teacher and Haim's parents will call the learning consultant at any time during the school year if problems arise, or if additional strategies seem necessary.

Appendix H

Role-Playing Situations for Workshop III

(These are the same situations found on page 196 of the *tzadikim* guide and may be copied for distribution to *tzadikim* pairs.)

Every time Ms. Gold introduces a new activity, Ronny, your first-grade student, seems as if he is lost in space. Your learning plan suggests that you repeat directions to him. When the teacher gives directions, you try to do this, but he still seems to still be lost. This time, you decide to . . .

Your learning plan suggests that you take your second grader, Leslie, for short walks as frequent breaks to help her refocus. She loves going on walks with you; however, you find that her time out of the classroom seems to actually cause her to have more problems reorienting and focusing on the activity at hand once you get back in the classroom. Upon reentering the classroom this time, you . . .

Michael, your third-grade student, tells you that he is embarrassed that you always sit right next to him. He asks if you can sit in the back of the classroom instead. You're not sure you will be able to utilize your assigned strategies if you are so far away, but you also want to respect his feelings. So you . . .

Allison seems to be falling significantly behind in Hebrew class. You are following all the suggestions in her learning plan, but she is not learning any of the Hebrew letters and you are growing concerned. Her second-grade year is now more than half over. As you are working today, you decide to . . .

Dylan is the only pre-K student in the class who can't sit still. His learning plan states that when Dylan is fidgety, he should be allowed to move around. Mrs. Wasser has asked you to try to keep him in his seat. Nothing you try seems to work. At this point, you . . .

Appendix I

Tzadik(ah) Evaluation

Name: ______________________________

When he/she works with his/her student, I notice:

He/she is particularly good at:

I notice that he/she struggles with:

Adjectives or words I would use to describe his/her leadership style or skills (use Jewish concepts, if possible):

Areas where I have noticed his/her growth or "aha" moments I have witnessed in his/her work as a *tzadik(ah)*:

References

Address, R. F., and M. Hochman, M., eds.. 2000. ***Al Pi Darco: According to Their Ways.*** New York: UAHC. Print.

Aylor, M., Garriott, P., and Snyder, L. Summer 2001. "Inclusion Confusion: Putting the Pieces Together." ***Teacher Education and Special Education.*** Online. Available via Wilson Select Plus.

Dupuis, Bonnie, MA. "Does Inclusion Help Students?: Perspectives from Regular Education and Students with Disabilities." Online. http://www.naset.org/782.0.html .

Goldstein, J. L., and C. N. Levine. Spring 2000. *Consortium of Special Educators in Central Agencies for Jewish Education,* 2–13.

Halvorsen, A. T., and T. Neary. 2001. ***Building Inclusive Schools: Tools and Strategies for Success.*** PUB CITY (Boston?): Allyn & Bacon.

McLaughlin, V., P. Rea, and C. Walther-Thomas. Winter 2002. "Outcomes for Students with Learning Disabilities in Inclusive and Pullout Programs." ***Exceptional Children.*** Online. Available via WilsonSelectPlus.

The Workshops

Before You Begin

You have chosen a righteous path for this coming year. Over the coming months, as you complete this course with your supervisor, you will develop and learn skills for assisting a student with special needs. Through these workshops, you will be exposed to the terminology of learning differences and learn to utilize strategies helping students succeed in the classroom. Most of all, you will develop a relationship with an individual and make a lasting impact on his or her life.

Before attending each workshop, you are required to do some home study. These assignments (called Self-Study Exercises) are designed to prepare you for the discussions that will take place with your workshop facilitator. Although they do not require any research, please take these self-studies seriously. You should set aside about half an hour at least one week in advance of the workshop sessions. The day before the workshop, review your answers and make any necessary changes or additions to your work. Be sure to carefully write out all your answers, as they will be used to guide discussions in the workshops.

There is a famous story about a little boy on a beach who was picking up starfish from the shore and throwing them back into the sea one by one. An older man walking by saw the boy working tirelessly and looked beyond him at thousands of starfish that had also been washed up on the shore. When he approached the boy, he asked, "Young man, what are you doing?" The boy answered, "I am throwing these fish back in the sea before they dry up and die." The man replied, "But young man, for every fish you throw back in, there are a thousand more washing up on shore. What difference can you possibly make?" The little boy bent down again, continuing his business of picking up one starfish at a time and hurling it back into the sea, and answered, "I made a difference for this one . . . and this one . . . and this one . . ."

As you go about your sacred work this year, may you come to see the impact you will make on your student with every small act of kindness.

B'hatzlacha (good luck)!

Part 1

Learning to Be a *Tzadik*:

Stepping Up to Make a Change in the World

Workshop I

Notes

WORKSHOP I

Self-Study Exercises

(to be completed prior to attending Workshop I)

Think of a situation when you were learning a new skill and write it below. An example of this may be learning to swim, ride a bike, or skate. What were some of the basic skills you needed to know in order to succeed? Examples for swimming are "holding your breath," "kicking," etc.

New skill: ______________________________

____

____

____

____

____

____

Basic skills needed to succeed at this: ______________________________

____

____

____

____

____

____

____

____

____

____

____

____

____

As you probably remember, learning a new skill takes patience, practice, and concentration. In acquiring most new skills, we succeed within a relatively short time. As with all new endeavors, we begin by building on skills we have previously learned. For example, before we learned to read, we learned the letters and their sounds, and before we learned how to play baseball, we learned how to run, throw and catch a ball, swing a bat, and so on. But, if we do not have the basic skills (such as knowledge of the letters or how to throw a ball), learning more complex skills is nearly impossible.

Not all children learn basic skills at the same pace and many children are born without the ability to learn basic skills easily. For most of us, crawling and walking came naturally within our first eighteen months. Yet there are many babies and toddlers who must work with physical and occupational therapists to teach them these basic skills.

Think back to your childhood. Are there any basic skills that were difficult for you to learn? What are some skills that are still challenging for you?

Basic skills that were hard for you to learn:___________________________

____

____

____

____

____

____

____

Skills that are still challenging for you: ___________________________

____

____

____

____

____

____

____

____

____

The students you will be working with over the next year are not typical learners. Though outsiders may or may not easily recognize their differences, each of these students learns or develops at a different pace than their peers. Some of these students don't even recognize that they are different from their peers. Your role is to assist these students by utilizing strategies that are designed to remove many of the barriers that hinder their learning and allow them to participate in Jewish learning alongside their peers. During the upcoming workshop, you will learn about some common learning differences that you may encounter.

Throughout your life, you have probably seen or met individuals with disabilities or learning differences. Think of a specific person you have encountered in the past (in person or on television or in the movies).

1. When you saw him or her, how did you feel? Carefully describe your emotions.

2. Do you know what type of disability or learning difference he or she has? If so, what is it?

3. What questions do you have about his or her differences?

In religious school, you studied the holidays, history, and traditions of Judaism. If you became a bar or bat mitzvah, you probably began studying commentaries on the Torah and other Jewish texts. Our great Sages have been commenting on and discussing our heritage and traditions for thousands of years.

As with most topics, Judaism has a lot to say about those who learn differently. During the first workshop, you will explore what our tradition says about this. Before we study it as a group, think about some of the precepts and stories you learned about Judaism.

What do you think that Jewish tradition says about how we should treat those who are different? Describe at least one idea or story from our tradition that deals with differences. Feel free to list any quotes from the Bible or commentators, if you remember them.

In the Passover seder, we are reminded about how to treat others, because we were once strangers in the Land of Egypt. The goal of the seder is to reenact the experience of our ancestors' slavery in Egypt. Similarly, the key to becoming a successful mentor to a student with special needs is understanding learning differences and how they affect students. Your knowledge of these differences will assist you in becoming an empathetic leader.

Are there any learning differences with which you are already familiar? Name one or more and attempt to describe how they affect children.

Learning difference: ______________________________

____

____

____

____

How it affects the child: ______________________________

____

____

____

____

Learning difference: ______________________________

____

____

____

____

How it affects the child: ______________________________

____

____

____

____

Notes

WORKSHOP I

Part 1: What Is a *Tzadik(ah)*?

Objectives: By the end of this workshop, you will be able to:

- Understand the meaning of the words *tzadik, tzadikah, tzadikim,* and *tzadikot* and use these words correctly.
- Outline the roles of *tzadikim*.
- Understand what *tzadikim* do in the classroom.
- Describe the centrality of helping others in Jewish tradition.

Who Are *Tzadikim*?

In the Israelites' quest to become a holy people, deserving of entering the Promised Land, Moses instructs them, "Justice, justice shall you pursue" (Deuteronomy 16:2). In Hebrew, the word for "justice" is *tzedek,* and those who work to bring a greater measure of justice to the world are called *tzadikim.* Throughout our tradition, Jews have striven to act righteously. The Talmud teaches that in every generation there are thirty-six righteous people (called *lamed-vavniks,* from the Hebrew letters *lamed* and *vav* that represent the number thirty-six) who are ordinary, humble, and hidden among us. God allows the world to continue to exist because these *lamed-vav tzadikim* are living in our community and sustaining us without our even knowing it.

Today, you begin your journey as a *tzadik* or *tzadikah.* Like *tzadikim* in the generations before us, you too have a unique challenge to pursue justice in the world. As a religious school *tzadik* or *tzadikah,* you will bring justice to our world by helping a child who was born with a special need succeed in Jewish learning. As a trained teaching assistant working individually with students with special needs, you will make sure your students are not stigmatized or separated from their peers. Though your students need one-on-one assistance in their learning, it is our goal to make sure that they do not feel any different than the rest of the students in their class. Though you may have additional *madrichim,* or assistants, working in your school, your team's specialized skills will blend in with the rest of the school. Yet you will learn that without you and your specialized teaching methods, classroom learning cannot succeed. Like the *lamed-vav tzadikim,* you will help sustain the overall success of the class. Thus with the righteous work you are about to embark on, you are taking on the name and the goal of *tzadikim.*

But before you begin, it is important to learn to use the Hebrew word for "righteous one" correctly. A male is called a *tzadik* (צַדִּיק) and a female is called a *tzadikah* (צַדִּיקָה). The plural of *tzadik* is *tzadikim* (צַדִּיקִים) and the feminine plural is *tzadikot* (צַדִּיקוֹת).

Rachel and Lily are called ______________________________.

Michael is a ______________________________________.

Robert and Jill are __________________________________.

Beth is a ____.

The Role of *Tzadikim*

Though every day may be different working with your student, you are charged with certain responsibilities that will help your student succeed. Just as you move to a certain rhythm in the way you interact in the world, you must also learn the MUSIC of becoming an effective *tzadik* or *tzadikah:*

M odeling skills and behavior
U nderstanding your student's needs
S tudent advocacy
I mplementing behavioral management
C ommunicating with parents

The most effective *tzadikim* model techniques for learning, understand their student's needs, advocate for their student in the classroom, assist with behavior management, and maintain constant communication with their student's parents. Through the next few exercises, you will begin to learn the MUSIC of being a righteous one.

Modeling

If you have been a *madrich* or *madrichah* (a classroom assistant) in your religious school, you know the importance of being a role model for your students. *Madrichim* learn that modeling respectful behavior and other positive actions teach students how to act in the classroom. As a *tzadik* or *tzadikah*, you should always model techniques that will assist students in successful learning. For example, when you read Hebrew, you should use your finger to follow along. This helps you focus on the individual word or syllable that you are reading. Though you may read Hebrew well without using your finger, modeling this strategy will make the action seem more natural for your student. In addition, other students in the class may pick up on your behavior and also begin to use this strategy.
If you are assigned to work with a boy who has hearing problems (even with a hearing aid), what are some simple behaviors that you could model to help him succeed in class? (Think about his seating location, what he should do when others are speaking, etc.)

____

____

Understanding

All children are different and have different learning and physical needs. In this workshop, almost everyone is processing the lesson differently. Some people in the room learn better by hearing the information verbally and others must read it or see it to understand it. A few people in the room may have "photographic memories" and can memorize all the details on the page, while others may be color-blind, thus affecting the way colored texts and pictures look to them. If you have ever recorded your voice on a phone or a digital recorder, you will notice that it sounds different to you when you play it back. This is a simple way of understanding how others may hear things differently.

- ***Empathy Challenge***

Your facilitator is going to give you a mirror and a pencil. Have a partner place the mirror just to the left of the star on the line so that the star will reflect into the mirror. Looking only at the star in the mirror, trace the star with your pencil.

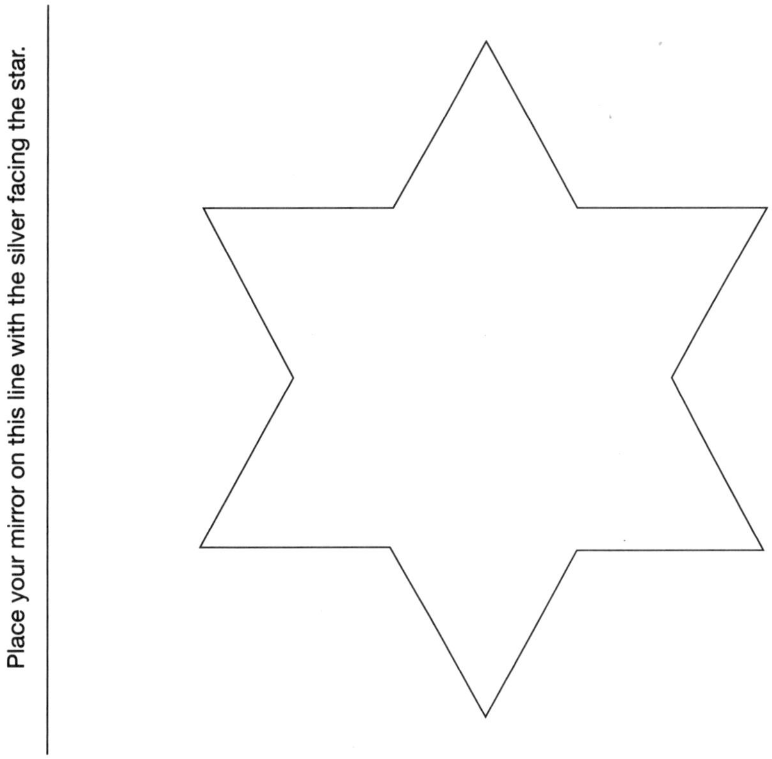

Place your mirror on this line with the silver facing the star.

When you have finished tracing the star, have your partner complete the same exercise.

(Answer the following question after both of you have completed the exercise)

How well did you do? Describe how you felt as you were trying to trace the star. ____

____

____

____

This exercise was a simple example to show you how it feels to learn differently. When it was over, you were able to remove the mirror and go back to "normal." Think about what it would feel like if your perception and vision were always like this. What would it be like playing baseball, eating candy out of a small bag, or reading a book?

When you spend time with your student over the next year, try to imagine what it would be like to live with his or her needs every day. You may wish to use the pages in the back of this book to write down thoughts and feelings as your experience them.

Student Advocacy

Living with a learning difference not only makes everyday tasks and learning challenging, it also makes interacting in the world more difficult. Many special needs are not seen by the outside world. For example, when a child has difficulty hearing, people often think he or she is rude because he or she does not respond when someone says "hello."

As a *tzadik* or *tzadikah*, it is your responsibility to advocate, or stand up, for your student. For example, when a teacher plays a game, randomly calling on students to read from their books, a student with learning needs may not process the request at the same speed as the other students. Oftentimes, this will cause embarrassment as the other children in the class giggle, make condescending comments, or pressure him or her to answer.

If your teacher plays a game like this regularly in class, and you notice this happening to your student, what would you do to advocate for him or her?

____

____

____

____

____

Implementing Behavior Management

Oftentimes, there is a correlation between special needs and negative behavior patterns. Some children with learning needs are active and cannot focus on the activity at hand. Other children cannot keep up with the "regular" pace of the class and therefore are constantly reprimanded for not following directions. Still other students' minds operate at such high levels that they get bored and move ahead to another thought before the teacher finishes explaining the lesson at hand. They subsequently get blamed for not paying attention.

Though these children disrupt the normal flow in the classroom, most of the time their negatively perceived behaviors are not their fault. As a *tzadik* or *tzadikah*, it is your role to assist your student in managing his or her behavior. This can be done in a variety of ways, but mostly it is accomplished by creating a behavior management system. Star charts, rewards, and regular reminders (nonverbal cues, such as a wink, a tap on the shoulder, etc.) are all systems that can be set up by *tzadikim*. The most important thing to remember is that behavior management should always be positive to promote positive behavior.

Think back to your own childhood. What kind of positive reward system(s) did your parents or your teachers create for you? Describe a system like this and how you felt when you succeeded. ______________

____

____

____

____

____

____

Communicating with Parents

Your final role as a *tzadik* or *tzadikah* is to be the link between the school and the parents. Parents of students with special needs often need additional support and reinforcement from their children's teachers. Because the classroom teacher is responsible for communicating with all parents of students in the class, he or she often does not have the time to communicate sufficiently with the parents of those with special needs. As a *tzadik* or *tzadikah*, you are charged with the additional responsibility of supporting your child's parents.

If you are going to be absent, it is crucial for you to let your student's parents (and your program coordinator) know, so that alternate arrangements can be made. Also, when you notice that a particular strategy is successful with your student, you should let the child's parents know so that they can utilize that strategy at home and share that strategy with the teacher(s) in the child's weekday school. Alternatively, if your strategies are not working, a parent can be a good source of assistance and support in finding another strategy that may work better for your student. Whatever the communication involves, it is important to remember that communication with parents should always be positive, even if the day was not a successful one for the student.

Give an example of a positive communication that you might share with parents about their child. (This can be a comment about the student's behavior, interactions with the teacher or other students, or about his or her class work.) ____

____

____

____

____

____

____

____

____

Judaism and Helping Others

About 3,700 years ago, when three visitors appeared at their tent, Abraham and Sarah modeled a behavior that would set a high standard for the future of Judaism. Rather than letting the strangers suffer in the heat of the desert, they invited them into their tent for water, cake, and rest. This is the origin of the Jewish value of welcoming the stranger.

Abraham's care for others was also shown when he argued with God in order save the people of Sodom and Gomorrah. Unlike those who came before him, he risked his life for others by challenging God on their behalf: "Will you sweep away the innocent along with the guilty? Shall not the Judge of all the earth deal justly?" (Genesis 18:23, 25) Through Abraham's model of care for others, our tradition has taught the importance of hospitality and looking out for the stranger.

Ever since the days of Abraham and Sarah, our texts and the leaders of our people have stood up for equality and fair treatment of others. The *Tanach* (the Hebrew Bible), our sacred writings, and our Sages have all shared insights on this subject.

Read over the Jewish texts on the left side of the page and try to match them to the interpretations on the right.

A **You shall not . . . place a stumbling block before the blind. Leviticus 19:14**	1 A synagogue should be a place where all people are welcomed.
B **Look not at the container but at what it contains. Pirkei Avot 4:27**	2 We should always make sure that others get the same respect that we do, no matter who they are.
C **For My house shall be called a house of prayer for all peoples. Isaiah 56:7**	3 Sometimes there is something special hidden inside a person that may not be easily seen from the outside.
D **All your children shall be students of Adonai. Isaiah 54:13**	4 You should treat everyone the same way that you hope to be treated.
E **All of Israel is responsible for one another. Shavuot 39a**	5 God will not look favorably in the future on those who make fun of or shame others.
F **Let your friend's honor be as precious to you as your own. Pirkei Avot 2:10**	6 If someone is at a disadvantage, we should be careful not to make his or her way any more difficult.
G **One who... publicly shames a fellow human being..., that person would have no portion in the world to come. Pirkei Avot 3:11**	7 All Jewish children shall be given the opportunity to study Judaism.
H **Love your neighbor as yourself. Leviticus 19:18**	8 As Jews, we should take care of all of our people.

Notes

WORKSHOP I

Part 2: Understanding Learning Differences and Learning Plans

Objectives: By the end of this workshop, you will be able to:

- Understand descriptions of key learning differences.
- Interpret the basic information in a learning plan.
- Describe your student's learning needs.

Understanding Different Types of Special Needs

Students with special needs may learn differently for a variety of reasons. Some may have difficulty with their fine-motor skills, which means they may have trouble cutting out a picture or writing with a regular pencil. Some students may have trouble listening to the teacher and following directions, not because they are misbehaving, but rather because they have difficulty understanding what is being said. Some students may not be able to pay attention for long periods of time, while other students may have no trouble listening but be unable to remember the specific sound associated with a Hebrew letter.

- ***Empathy Challenge***

Work with a partner. Read the following instructions to your partner and ask him or her to do exactly what you say. Speak at a normal speed, no faster or slower than you would normally speak:

"Find a blank page in either your book or in your backpack. Number the page from one to ten. Next to number three write down your favorite color, your favorite food next to number four, and next to number ten write down the person in Jewish history who means the most to you. Also, make sure that you write your first, last, and middle names and your age and grade on the top right-hand corner of the page. Next to number five, write the names of three Hebrew letters, and in the remaining blanks write five things you want for Chanukah. When you finish, turn your page over and raise your hand."

Discuss the following questions with your partner:

When you were trying to follow the directions, how did you feel and why?

____

____

____

____

____

How would you feel if you were listening to these directions in the classroom and you were the only student who appeared not to be able to follow along with your teacher?

____

____

____

____

____

Students who learn differently have usually had an evaluation by a doctor, a psychologist, or a therapist specializing in their particular area of weakness. After a full evaluation has been completed, the parents are typically given a copy of the professional's report. The report includes a diagnosis that helps the parents better understand their child's particular needs. In addition, the report usually includes recommendations for therapy programs to help the child, special school services needed, and specific strategies for the child's teacher. Some of these children may go to a special private school or they may attend a public school and go to special education classes for all or part of their day. Children in the public schools often have what is called an IEP, or an individualized education program. An IEP includes specific strategies that should be used in the classroom to help the teacher ensure that the child succeeds.

Below is a list of common special needs that you may encounter in the *tzadikim* program. The purpose of this information is to help you become familiar with some of the most common types of special needs that are seen in children today. The definitions and examples do not provide a full picture of these complex diagnoses and are not intended to be used to help you diagnose students yourself. They are only intended to provide you with examples of manifestations of learning needs that you may encounter in your work as a *tzadik* or *tzadikah*.

Attention-Deficit/Hyperactivity Disorder (ADHD): Students diagnosed with ADHD exhibit some or all of the following symptoms: inattention, distractibility, impulsivity, and hyperactivity.

- Inattention and distractibility mean the student has trouble focusing. *Example*: While the teacher is talking, Josh is staring at the Sukkot decorations on the bulletin board and he is listening to the noise in the hallway as the kindergarten class is walking to the library.
- Impulsivity causes students to deviate from classroom rules. *Example*: Jacob frequently yells out questions without raising his hand.
- Hyperactivity leads a child to have difficulty sitting for prolonged periods of time. *Example*: Michael is squirming in his seat while the rest of the third graders are sitting quietly.

Auditory Processing Disorder (APD): Students diagnosed with APD have difficulty understanding what they hear, even when they are trying their best to listen. They are often misidentified as having behavioral problems.

- *Example*: The frustrated teacher repeats three times for Jacob to turn to page 52 and subsequently yells at him for not paying attention, but Jacob does not have the ability to follow oral commands.

Autism: Students diagnosed with autism have difficulty with social interactions and communication. Depending on the severity of the condition, students with autism may not speak or may have a very limited vocabulary. They tend to have a difficult time in novel surroundings, such as a Sunday school classroom. They also have a hard time looking people in the eye. A related, less severe diagnosis is called Asperger syndrome.

- *Example*: Micah, who has Asperger syndrome, attends the weekend overnight fourth-grade retreat, but he appears as if he is in his own world, while the rest of the students interact with one another and their teachers.

Developmental Delays: Students diagnosed with developmental delays have not reached benchmarks for development in one or several of these areas: intelligence, language/speech, physical development, social/emotional development, and self-help skills. Down syndrome and cerebral palsy are examples of two disorders associated with developmental delays.

1 Hyperactivity takes many different forms in different children. While having trouble sitting still is a common example, it can also be exhibited through other behaviors, such as restlessness, fidgeting, or the constant touching of objects and people.

- Students with intellectual delays have difficulty learning at the same rate as their peers.
  Example: You are trying to teach Shayna that the letter *bet* sounds like *B*. You have gone over it with her multiple times. Once you begin teaching her the next letter, *gimel*, Shayna has already forgotten the sounds a *bet* makes.
- Students with speech or language delays may have trouble saying certain sounds, making their speech hard to understand, or they may have difficulty expressing what they want to say because they have a limited vocabulary.
  Example: You are trying to teach the difference between *shin* and *sin* to Chelsea, who has a speech delay. When she pronounces the letters, they both sound like the letter *S*.
- Students with physical delays may have gross-motor delays, meaning they cannot walk well or they may be in a wheelchair. Students with fine-motor delays may have difficulty using their hands.
  Example: Jonathan cannot complete an art project because he cannot hold scissors properly.
- Students with social/emotional delays may be socially immature, compared to the other children in their class, and they will subsequently have difficulty making friends or even just initiating a conversation with a peer.
  Example: Lori, a sixth-grade student, always sits by herself during break, playing with her stuffed animals, while the other girls laugh and talk about boys and movies.
- Students with delays in the self-help area have difficulty taking care of themselves.
  Example: Ashley needs help pulling down her pants so she can go the bathroom.

Dyslexia: Dyslexia is a language-based learning disability that may interfere with a child's ability to learn written and oral language, including reading. Students with dyslexia often have a hard time decoding (sounding out words), writing legibly, spelling, and reading, especially if they are asked to read aloud. When they are reading, they may encounter visual-perception problems. These students often have a difficult time learning how to read Hebrew and English.

- *Example*: When Alex is reading Hebrew, he complains that the words look as though they are moving on the page.

Learning Disabilities (LDs): Students diagnosed with a learning disability have normal intelligence, but they may struggle in one or more of the following areas: oral expression, listening comprehension, written expression, basic reading skills, and/or math calculation and reasoning. Depending on the type of learning disability they have, children may display a variety of different symptoms in the classroom.

- *Example:* Maggie has difficulty formulating her thoughts and the wrong words keep coming out when she is telling the class what she did for the Passover holiday.

Sensory Integration (SI) Issues: Students diagnosed with SI issues have difficulty processing everyday sensations, such as noises or touch. They may also exhibit unusual behaviors, such as avoiding or seeking out touch, movement, sounds, and sights.

- *Example*: Evan becomes abnormally scared when he hears the high-pitched sound of the fire alarm during a fire drill.

Tourette Syndrome: Tourette syndrome is a neurological disorder that causes tics. These are unwanted twitches, movements, or sounds that people make. Though children may have tics without having Tourette syndrome, children are only diagnosed with this condition when they have two tics that affect body movement and one that is a sound (all observed over the course of at least one year). Although children with Tourette syndrome may seem disrespectful, their tics are involuntary and may include inappropriate language or curse words.

Applying What You Learned

Mrs. Goldman is beginning her lesson. All of her first-grade students are sitting in their seats and enthusiastically listening as Mrs. Goldman tells the story of Jonah and the whale. All her students are sitting, that is, except for Mark. Mark is moving around his seat and his eyes are darting all over the room. He suddenly blurts out, "I saw a whale once when I went to SeaWorld with my Mommy and Daddy last year. It was really big!"

What symptoms did Mark exhibit? ______________________

____

____

____

____

Although we should never attempt to label or diagnose a student, given the symptoms above, does Mark display behaviors similar to any of the special needs you just learned about? If so, which one(s)? ____________

____

____

____

____

> Ms. Kushner is having the students in her third-grade Sunday school class each take a turn reading from their textbooks about Shabbat traditions. Sarah asks to go to the bathroom when it is her turn to read. She looks as if she is about to cry. The teacher asks a teaching assistant to go with Sarah. When they get into the hallway, Sarah bursts into tears and says, "I can't read out loud in front of the entire class. Everyone will think that I am so stupid! The words look funny on the page. I hate Sunday school!"

What were Sarah's issues and how did they make her feel about coming to Sunday school? ____________________________

____

____

____

____

Were any of the special needs described above unfamiliar to you? If so, which one(s)? ____________________________

____

____

1. ____

____

2. ____

____

Understanding the Student You Will Be Shadowing

Students with special needs often have a one-on-one facilitator in a classroom to help them participate in classroom activities. These facilitators are typically called "shadows." As a *tzadik* or *tzadikah*, you may be assigned to one student whom you will shadow in the classroom. Some *tzadikim* will be assigned more than one student, especially if there are two students with mild learning differences who are in the same class. Other *tzadikim* may be assistants to the supervisor of the program, and may work with multiple students outside of their regular Sunday school class in order to provide specialized one-on-one Hebrew tutoring. If you are a *tzadik* or *tzadikah* assigned to more than one student, you must understand the specific needs of each one of your students.

Ideally, your synagogue's program supervisor will provide you with a learning plan for your student. Learning plans have two parts. The first part describes what learning problems your assigned student are having. The second part provides specific classroom management strategies. The purpose of this workshop session is to ensure that you understand how to interpret the first part of a learning plan.

Please note that your synagogue's resources may not allow for a full learning plan as outlined in this book. Instead, you may be provided with a psychological report or an individualized education program (IEP) from the student's secular school. An IEP includes information about how your student learns and specific classroom management strategies, as well as information that will not be applicable to what you are doing in the classroom (specific special education services, therapies, and goals, for example). If your program supervisor does not have any written information for you, he or she may just give you information verbally.

Applying What You Learned

LEARNING PLAN FOR LINDSAY (PART 1)

Lindsay has a medical condition that causes developmental delays. such as walking, cutting, holding a pencil, speaking, and understanding classroom content. She has had no behavior problems over the last two years at Sunday school. She enjoys music and is able to attend the music activities without much supervision. Lindsay has delayed social skills and thus has difficulty initiating social contact with her peers. She has successfully participated in class with the assistance of a student from the *tzadikim* program for three years, and she enjoys the individualized attention. When Hebrew phonics were introduced at a more accelerated pace, her *tzadik* took her out of the classroom and worked one-on-one with Lindsay to help her learn and review Hebrew letters. It is not expected that Lindsay will be able to learn all the skills being taught this year, and she will be having an adapted bat mitzvah ceremony. So the teacher should not worry if Lindsay is learning the same amount of Hebrew as the other students. The goal is for Lindsay to continue to have a positive experience on Sundays.

After reading the above information, what are three important things you should note about Lindsay?

1. ______________________________
2. ______________________________
3. ______________________________

What are your initial thoughts about how you might be able to help Lindsay successfully participate in some of her class activities?

____
____
____
____
____

Wisdom from Our Sages

Our Rabbis taught: A minor who knows how to shake the *lulav* is subject to the obligation of the *lulav*; [if he knows how] to wrap himself [in a tallit], he is subject to the obligation of *tzitzit*; [if he knows how] to lay *t'fillin*, his father must acquire *t'fillin* for him; if he is able to speak, his father must teach him Torah and the reading of the *Sh'ma*.

Sukkah 42a

Based on a translation in Ivan G. Marcus, *The Jewish Life Cycle: Rites of Passage from Biblical to Modern Times.*

Thousands of years ago, our Sages taught in the Talmud about the obligation of children to perform the mitzvot of shaking the lulav on Sukkot, wearing a tallit and laying t'fillin, and learning Torah and reciting the Sh'ma.

At the end of the passage above, what is a child's father required to do if his child is able to speak? ______________________________

____
____

Does the text mention a particular age to begin teaching? ___________

How is this text different from what you have learned about the obligation to perform mitzvot beginning at the age of bar or bat mitzvah?

____

____

____

____

____

From this text we learn that we must teach Torah and mitzvot even to those who are not obligated to perform the commandments, no matter what their age. Likewise, just as we are obligated to teach Torah to our youngest children, so, too, we are obligated to teach Torah to every student.

The Talmud tells the story of Rabbi Peraida, who had to teach a student a lesson four hundred times before he understood it. During the teaching, Rabbi Peraida took a break to perform a mitzvah. When he returned to continue teaching the student the lesson four hundred times, the student explained that he could not understand it because of the interruption. Therefore, Rabbi Peraida started over again, teaching the student another four hundred times until he understood. Suddenly, a heavenly voice shouted out that Rabbi Peraida and his generation merited a place in the world-to-come. (from Eruvin 54b)

What do you learn from the story of Rabbi Peraida? ________________

____

____

____

____

____

____

Read a copy of your student's learning plan. If your supervisor does not have a written plan for you, he or she may provide you with information in a different way. Please take a moment to read the information that describes your student's specific special needs.

Use the space below to write down two or three facts about your student that you feel are important:

1. ______________________________

2. ______________________________

3. ______________________________

4. ______________________________

5. ______________________________

What questions do you have for your supervisor about your student?

1. ______________________________

2. ______________________________

3. ______________________________

4. ______________________________

5. ______________________________

WORKSHOP I

Part 3: Classroom Strategies for the Child Who Learns Differently

Objectives: By the end of this workshop, you will be able to:

- Understand a variety of classroom and individualized teaching strategies for teaching students with special needs.
- Identify specific strategies for your student's success in the classroom.
- Interpret and summarize the second part of your student's learning plan.
- Begin to model skills and behaviors for your student.

Understanding Classroom Strategies

Children with attention or processing difficulties, such as students with ADHD or an auditory processing disorder, have difficulty listening or paying attention in class. Certain learning disabilities also affect the ability to listen, as explained earlier. Now that you understand why these students have difficulty listening, you can begin to learn how to help them in class. The following are a list of classroom strategies to help children who have difficulty listening. These strategies will not be necessary for all children who learn differently, but they will generally be helpful if you are working with a student who has difficulty listening or focusing. As you begin working with your student, you should experiment with each of these strategies to see which works best.

1. Keep directions short and simple, and speak slowly.
2. Frequently repeat directions to the student.
3. Have the student repeat the directions back to you.
4. Use gestures (hand motions and body language) when providing directions.
5. Make sure that you and your student are sitting within close proximity of the teacher.
6. Use visuals whenever possible, such as writing directions down on paper as you say them or pointing to the word that the teacher is reading.
7. Give breaks often. If the student seems to be having problems focusing, allow him or her to take a break. Examples include taking a short walk or going to the library to read a book.
8. Review classroom rules with your student.
9. Use positive reinforcement. Create a positive reinforcement behavior management system using stars or happy faces. (Example, if Jamie gets

three stars by the end of Sunday school, he can visit the computer lab at the end of the day).

10. Show enthusiasm.
11. Don't fight the impossible. If hyperactivity is an issue for your student, simply ignore the child moving around or squirming in his or her seat.
12. Constantly offer praise. Comment on the student's positive behaviors as much as possible. Provide positive attention and positive reinforcement. Every child deserves praise each day!
13. Keep in mind that saying "sssh" is ineffective.
14. Use nonverbal cues to stop inappropriate behaviors (such as a nod, a tap on the shoulder, waving a finger, etc.).

Understanding Individualized Teaching Strategies for Hebrew Learning

Your student may have difficulty learning Hebrew for a variety of reasons. As a *tzadik* or *tzadikah,* you may be asked to work one-on-one with your student to help with Hebrew learning, and some *tzadikim* work as assistants providing Hebrew tutoring to a variety of students with learning differences, instead of working as classroom shadows.

Many students with special needs are not able to learn using traditional teaching methods. They may attend special schools or special education classes in their public schools. Many of these schools or classes provide specialized teaching for these children using multisensory teaching methods. This means that students may learn using their senses, such as tactile (touch) or visual (sight) cues.

- ***Empathy Challenge***

Read the following instructions and try to follow them exactly.

1. Write your name on tde dottom left-hanb corner of tdis pope in all lower-case letters.

S. Adove your name, braw tdree stars inside a circle.

3. On tde tog of tde qage, write the name of your weekboy school.

P. When you finisd, lox your heab on your besk.

How did you feel when completing this activity and why?

____

____

____

____

How would you feel if you were asked to complete the directions above in a short amount of time? How would you feel if your teacher was angry with you for "not trying" after you were unable to complete the activity?

____

____

____

____

Learning Hebrew can be a challenge. When a child has a reading-based learning difference, learning Hebrew is even more challenging. The activity above gives you a brief experience of what these children deal with on a daily basis.

Basic Strategies for Teaching Hebrew to Students with Learning Differences

Here are some strategies that may be helpful to you when teaching Hebrew to a child who learns differently:

1. When teaching a letter that looks similar to another letter (e.g., *resh* and *dalet* or *chet* and *tav*), point out their similarities and differences by writing the letters side by side.
2. Have students use tactile exercises, such as molding the letters out of clay, pipe cleaners, or bendable wax sticks, so that they understand how the letters differ from each other.
3. Use fun mnemonic strategies (tricks to memorize) to help the student remember the sounds of letters and vowel sounds (such as the *resh* is more "rounded" than the *dalet*; its sound is *R*).
4. Enlarge the print size of the Hebrew text on a copy machine.
5. Remind your teacher not to call on students with reading-based learning differences to read out loud unless they volunteer.
6. Limit distractions from the page. (You can use self-adhesive notes to cover up pictures or other text on the sides of the page.)
7. Always have students read using their fingers or a pencil/pen to point to the words.

8. Segment (or break apart) syllables for the student. An ideal way to do this is by highlighting each syllable in alternating colors, as below:

בָּרוּךְ אַתָּה, יְיָ אֱלֹהֵינוּ, מֶלֶךְ הָעוֹלָם,
יוֹצֵר אוֹר וּבוֹרֵא חֹשֶׁךְ,

9. Provide simplified transliteration when appropriate. (For example, in *V'ahavta*, the word (insert Hebrew word here) is a tricky combination of sounds, so you may choose to write *"uv'shoch'b'ch"* above the text.)

- ***Empathy Challenge***

Read the following starting from the black arrow at the bottom left and then continuing going down from the white arrow. Then, continue reading alternating going up and down.

e	w	a	n	r	e		t	e	r
r		m	y	d	n	g	o	v	y
b	c			l		n			
e	a	o	p	i	a	i	l	e	f
H	n	t	e	h	n	y	e	h	i
			o	c	d	r	a	t	r
g	b	g	p			t	r		s
n	e	n	l	g	e		n	r	t
l		i	e	n	v	s		o	
d	c	g		i	e	t	H	f	t
a	h	n	i	d	n	l	e		i
e	a	e	n	u		u	b	w	m
R	l	l	c	l	a	d	r	e	e.

Now reread the above, this time using your finger to point to the words that you are trying to read to help you follow along.

Which time did you find it easier to read and understand the sentence above—using your finger or without using your finger? Why?

____

____

____

____

____

____

Explain how using a simple strategy can have a major impact on your ability to accomplish something basic.

____

____

____

____

____

____

____

Applying What You Learned

Remember Lindsay's learning plan (Part 1) from page 159? Take a minute to look back over this information.

What learning differences does Lindsay have? ____________________

____

Before reading Part 2 of her learning plan, discuss as a group what strategies you think might be effective for Lindsay.

LEARNING PLAN FOR LINDSAY (PART 2)

1. Lindsay will be provided with a special needs teaching assistant (from our *tzadikim* program) in class.
2. Both the teacher and the teaching assistant will help Lindsay with simple social exchanges with peers and her teacher.
3. Lindsay will be assisted with all classroom activities. The teacher and *tzadik(ah)* will help simplify those activities so Lindsay can participate. Alternative activities will be available (i.e., coloring pictures with a Judaic theme), if needed. During Hebrew time, she may go to the library to work one-on-one with her *tzadik(ah)*.
4. If needed as a behavioral distraction, Lindsay will be taken out of the class to walk around with her *tzadik(ah)* for approximately five to ten minutes. She will then come back to class and again participate.
5. The *tzadik(ah)* will provide one-on-one Hebrew instruction, utilizing the following strategies:
    - Limit distractions from the page.
    - Always have Lindsay read using her finger or a pencil/pen to point to the words.
    - Segment (or break apart) syllables.
6. Periods of time without the *tzadik(ah)* sitting next to her (such as during music or another engaging activity) should be attempted as appropriate.
7. The teacher/parents will call the learning consultant at any time during the school year if problems arise.

Wisdom from Our Sages

Human dignity is so important that it supersedes even a biblical prohibition.

Berachot 19b

What do you think this text from the Talmud means?

____

____

____

____

____

____

As you have been learning throughout this workshop, a major part of your job as a *tzadik(ah)* is to help your student feel "the same" as all other students in the school. In school settings, this is called "inclusion." Inclusion is a philosophy that all types of learners (including those with special needs) can be taught in the same classroom.

Judaism has always taught respect for others. Almost two thousand years ago, the Rabbis already began teaching the importance of preserving another human's dignity (in Hebrew this is called *kavod ha'briut*). *Kavod ha'briut* was so important to them that the ruling was made that one could break a law from the Torah in order to protect another person from embarrassment.

Can you think of a Jewish law that may need to be broken in order to protect someone's dignity? ______________________________

Have you ever wondered why saying the blessing before and after the Torah reading is called an *aliyah* and not the act of reading the Torah itself? The Rabbis knew that most people do not have the skills to read or chant Torah, so they appoint permanent readers for the text itself and then honor those who bless the reading. This is another form of *kavod ha'briut,* or avoiding embarrassment of others.

What simple acts of kavod ha'briut can you do to help your student avoid embarrassment? ______________________________

Understanding Strategies Needed to Help the Student You Will Be Mentoring

You have been given a learning plan or other information about the student you will be shadowing. Depending on what exactly your supervisor gave you, you may or may not have a list of strategies (similar to the format used for Lindsay above) to use with your student. If you have been given a specific learning plan, rewrite the strategies for your student now in your own words to help you better understand what you will be doing. If you have not been given specific strategies, use this as an opportunity to write your own learning plan, using the strategies outlined in this book and taking into consideration your student's specific special need.

Learning Plan Strategies for ________________ [your student's name]

1. ____________________________________

2. ____________________________________

3. ____________________________________

4. ____________________________________

5. ____________________________________

6. ____________________________________

7. ____________________________________

8. ____________________________________

List three ways you can model skills and behaviors for your student.

1. ____________________________________

2. ____________________________________

3. ____________________________________

Reward Chart for ______________________ [your student's name]

Tefilah	Hebrew Lesson	Music	Torah Lesson	Art

I earned _____ stars today!

Additional Comments: ____________________________________

____

____

Part 2

Continuing Education and Practical Training

Notes

WORKSHOP II

Self-Study Exercises

(to be completed prior to attending Workshop II)

By now you have had some time to get to know the student with whom you are working. At the last session, you were given a piece of paper with a description of a child with special needs. When you met the student you were assigned to shadow, however, you began to see a real person with feelings and emotions, not just words on a page.

Before your meeting, what did you expect your student to be like?

____

____

____

____

____

What were some of the differences from your expectations?

____

____

____

____

____

On your first day with your student, what were some of the hardest things for you? ______________________

____

____

____

____

____

What things were surprisingly easy? ______________________________

____

____

____

____

____

Look back a couple of pages and review some of the suggested strategies for working with your student. Which of these strategies worked well? Which did not work well?

Strategies that worked well: ______________________________

____

____

____

____

____

Strategies that did not work so well: ______________________________

____

____

____

____

____

In the time you have spent with your student, we hope that you have been able to connect with some of his or her feelings and emotions. Though sometimes it is hard to relate to someone so different from us, when we are in the role of caregiver, we typically connect with that person more easily. Like a parent relating to a child, the more we help someone, the less we come to see his or her differences.

Martin Buber, one of the greatest Jewish theologians of the twentieth century, spoke of two types of relationships: I-It and I-Thou. I-It relationships are basically those exchanges we have every day with store clerks, waiters, and others. They are characterized by a common need or a relationship of utility. For example, when I have finished picking out all my groceries, I go to the register and pay for them. The clerk rings them up and we have a brief conversation, yet it is typically a shallow conversation (characterized by remarks such as "It's really hot today" or "I can't believe the price of milk these days").

I-Thou relationships, on the other hand, are relationships between two people who care for each other. This can be with parents, a girlfriend or boyfriend, or even a teacher. In these encounters, both people care for the other person's welfare and needs, and both people fully accept each other. We think of these relationships as genuine.

Buber goes on to teach that when we have true I-Thou relationships, when both parties genuinely care for each other, God is present in the relationship and in these relationships, we can discover God.

Though you have only recently met your student, you are creating a caring relationship, similar to an I-Thou relationship. Do you feel a special connection to your student? If so, how does this make you feel? And, if not, what are some of the barriers that are keeping you from creating these special connections?

____

____

____

____

____

Before you forget, do you have any questions that you would like to ask your supervisor at the next session? Quickly jot them down.

1. ______________________________________

2. ______________________________________

3. ______________________________________

Notes

WORKSHOP II

The Invisible Need: Becoming a Classroom Advocate

Objectives: By the end of this workshop, you will be able to:

- Understand the importance of advocating for your student.
- Assist teachers in differentiating between behavioral needs and learning needs.
- Recognize additional learning needs in the classroom and be proactive in assisting the teacher.

Understanding the Importance of Advocating for Your Student

Now that you have had a couple of weeks of experience in the classroom, you have become acquainted with your student and some of his or her needs. In some of the challenging situations, you may have noticed that traditional teaching or classroom management does not work. At those junctures, you may have found strategies (like the ones you learned in the first workshop session) that work well. When you utilize the techniques on your learning plan or your own strategies, you are advocating for your student.

An advocate is someone who stands up or speaks out for the good of someone or something. Although you are becoming aware of and used to your student's special needs, the behaviors that he or she displays may be deemed inappropriate to the outside world. The more you work with your student, the more you are learning how to intervene when necessary. The next exercise is designed to help you become more comfortable with your new role as an advocate and to practice taking on this new role in other situations.

- ***Empathy Challenge: Advocating in Various Situations***

Divide up into three groups. Each group should take one of the three case studies below and answer the questions as a group. Pick a spokesperson and prepare to present your findings to the larger group.

Case Study 1

You are David's *tzadik* or *tzadikah*. David's Judaics teacher, Mrs. Cohen, has an intense lesson plan today. The children are reading from the text for a prolonged period and she is calling on different readers. The children are asked to sit quietly and wait for their turn to read. Mrs. Cohen is speaking in a monotone voice and is not introducing any new activities. Some of the students are laying their heads down on the desk, some are twirling their pencils or doodling, and others are staring off into space. A few are listening intently. David is fidgeting in his seat and keeps standing up and sitting down. At one point he gets up and walks around his desk in two circles, but then decides to sit back down. He soon begins to make funny noises that are distracting the students around him.

How would you feel sitting in Mrs. Cohen's classroom? ______________

____

____

____

____

What are some things going on in the classroom that may be making it difficult for David to sit quietly? ______________________________

____

____

____

____

If Mrs. Cohen were your student's teacher, we would recommend that you share some of David's difficulties in her class with your supervisor. What would you report to him or her? ______________________________

____

____

____

____

____

Case Study 2

You are Kayla's *tzadik* or *tzadikah*. Today Kayla's class is learning about Israel. Her teacher, Mr. Jacobs, loves to play a game called "Around the World." In this game, two students are asked to stand up at one time. Then they are asked a question about Israel. In order to move on to the next round of the game, one student must correctly answer the question before the other student. Kayla has played this game for the past two weeks and she always answers her questions incorrectly, so she doesn't advance. Today, when Mr. Jacobs announces that they are about to play the game, all the children in the class seem happy to play except for Kayla. She tells you that she needs to go to the bathroom. She seems very upset, so you go with her. As soon as she gets outside the classroom, Kayla starts to cry and says to you, "I hate this game. I never know the right answer because I'm so stupid. I don't want to go back to class."

If you were to ask Kayla how she is feeling in this class, what do you think she would say? ____________________

____

____

____

What are some of the things that make this game so frustrating for Kayla?

1. ____________________

2. ____________________

3. ____________________

If Mr. Jacobs were your student's teacher, we would recommend that you share some of Kayla's difficulties in his class with your supervisor. What would you report to him or her? ____________________

____

____

____

Case Study 3

You are Dylan's *tzadik* or *tzadikah*. Dylan loves the Judaics class, but when it is time for Hebrew, he becomes very anxious. His teacher, Ms. Hirsh, randomly calls on students to read out loud. Although Dylan's learning plan specifies that she not call on Dylan to read aloud in class because of his dyslexia, she seems to always forget. When Dylan is called on, the other students often laugh at him because he cannot recognize the letters and the teacher has to practically sound out the entire word for him. After class today, Dylan says to you, "I wish I was smart like the rest of the kids. I want to be able to read, too. I heard them laughing at me today!"

If you were to ask Dylan how he is feeling in this class, what do you think he would say? ____________________

____

____

____

____

What are some of the things that make this class frustrating for Dylan?

____

____

____

____

____

If Ms. Hirsh were your student's teacher, we would recommend that you share some of Dylan's difficulties in her class with your supervisor. What would you report to him or her?

____

____

____

____

Wisdom from Our Sages

> All of Israel is responsible for one another.
>
> Shavuot 39a

Although this short text from the Talmud seems simple, it has many different meanings in different contexts. Let's take it apart to better understand it. In Hebrew, the text reads Kol Yisrael (all of Israel). Who or what does "all of Israel" refer to? ______________________

____

____

____

____

____

____

In what ways are we, as Jews, responsible for one another? List at least five examples.

____

____

____

____

____

____

In Midrash Raba (Vayikra 4:6), the Rabbis tell the story of a man who is sitting in a boat with others. Suddenly, he takes out a hand drill and begins boring a hole in the bottom of the boat. When someone on the boat asks him what he is doing, he shrugs the man off, stating, "It's really none of your business." The man replies, "If the water begins to fill up our boat and we sink, not only will you go down, but we will all go down with you."

Looking more globally at our responsibility as Jews to help others, how might this story be compared to the work that you do as a tzadik(ah)?

____

____

____

____

____

____

____

____

____

Differentiating between Behavioral and Learning Needs

As an advocate for a child with attention or processing issues, you now know how his or her actions may often seem like true, intentional misbehaviors, rather than an actual inability to listen and comprehend what the teacher wants him or her to understand. Sometimes, however, you may be working with a child who displays poor behavioral choices and is utilizing a behavior management system such as those discussed in Workshop I (i.e., a star chart). It is important for you to continue to clearly understand the difference between a learning need and a behavioral need so you are able to properly employ the right strategy for the child with whom you are working. For example, if you are working with a child who is unable to follow lengthy instructions, due to attention or processing issues, and his or her teacher is constantly yelling at him or her for not listening, this is a clear example of a teacher not understanding the nature of the student's learning difference and genuine inability to understand and follow the teacher's instructions.

Think back to Workshop I. What were some strategies you learned to help a child with learning needs? List three below:

1. ____

2. ____

3. ____

Now consider specific strategies used for children with behavioral issues:

1. ____

2. ____

3. ____

Is it possible for some of these to overlap? Your answer should be yes! Many of the strategies that we learned in Workshop I can be applied to a child with both learning and behavioral needs. What is important to understand here, again, is your critical role as an advocate. We want to prevent, whenever possible, and intervene, when necessary, when our student's actions are being attributed solely to that fact that the student is "bad" or is constantly "not listening and misbehaving." We also want to help the teacher understand that we are dealing with a child who has very real issues listening and understanding what is being said to him or her.

Below is a list of events that may occur on a typical day with a child who learns differently. As you read through them, consider if each action displayed below reflects a behavioral or a learning need. Circle the one that you feel fits best or is more likely the better answer for each situation. You are not given full information on each item, so be creative and use your best judgment when deciding what you think may really be causing each student's actions.

1. Jason has dyslexia and is embarrassed to read aloud. He refuses to read out loud when the teacher calls on him.

   LEARNING NEED BEHAVIORAL NEED

2. Anna tells the teacher she doesn't want to read aloud because she forgot to do her homework over the last three weeks and she is additionally not prepared because she left her book at home.

   LEARNING NEED BEHAVIORAL NEED

3. Mark tells the substitute teacher that his name is Max because he thinks it's funny.

   LEARNING NEED BEHAVIORAL NEED

4. Lisa sits down and is the only one in class not participating in the art project because she cannot remember all the steps the teacher explained.

   LEARNING NEED BEHAVIORAL NEED

5. Mark, who is sitting in the desk behind Janie, knows that the teacher told him to mold his clay into a rectangle for the mezuzah art project, but he instead makes small little balls of clay which he is happily placing in Janie's long braid.

   LEARNING NEED BEHAVIORAL NEED

6. The teacher asks the class to open their books to page 9, complete numbers 1 through 5 at the top of the page, and then lay their heads down on their desks when they are done. Jason opens his book to page 5 and lays his head on the desk.

   LEARNING NEED BEHAVIORAL NEED

7. Mrs. Cohen tells Beth five times that a *resh* has a rounded edge and a *dalet* doesn't, but Beth continues to confuse them every time she tries to read a word with either letter.

   LEARNING NEED BEHAVIORAL NEED

8. Kevin's teacher keeps asking him to sit still in his seat, but he continues to wiggle in his chair.

   LEARNING NEED BEHAVIORAL NEED

9. Lawrence thinks it is funny to chew gum in class and then place his chewed gum under the desk when the teacher isn't looking.

   LEARNING NEED BEHAVIORAL NEED

10. Eric is trying to write the Hebrew word *Shabbat*, but his *bet* looks like a *tav*, and his *shin* looks more like an ant crawling with three legs. His friend sitting next to him laughs because he thinks Eric is trying to be funny by drawing the letters looking so "silly."

    LEARNING NEED BEHAVIORAL NEED

Review your answers as a group and discuss them. Discuss what really might be causing each of the students to display the behaviors described above.

Recognizing Additional Learning Needs in the Classroom

As you are learning to be an advocate for a child who learns differently, what happens when you notice another child in the same class who is displaying many of the behaviors that you learned about in Workshop I? If you are clearly noticing needs for this child, what happens when the teacher misses these needs? What happens if this child is constantly being reprimanded by the teacher, and you feel that there may be something else going on that is causing this child to constantly misbehave in the eyes of his or her teacher? What do you do? Can you advocate for another child with suspected learning needs? The answer is yes! However, you must be very careful to go through the proper avenues when trying to facilitate a positive change for the child you have been observing.

Below is a list of possible actions that you may take. Based on what you have learned until now, after each statement write "true" if you believe the statement describes an appropriate action for you as a tzadik(ah) to take, or write "false" if it does not.

Use the strategies suggested in your student's learning plan to write a learning plan for the other student in your class. Present the learning plan to the teacher. ____________________

Ask your rabbi, educator, or supervisor to come and observe the child in class.____________________

When the child is having trouble concentrating, take the initiative to take the other student outside for a walk in order to give him a break (since you know this works well for your student). ____________________

Ask the teacher if you can talk to him or her after class about what you are noticing with this child and some things that you think you might be able to do to help. Ask if you can try to help. ____________________

Find that child's parents and ask them if their child has a special need.

____

Now let's take a look at these questions more carefully:

1. As you have probably come to realize, your learning consultant spends a lot of time writing learning plans for each student with special needs. He or she has particular expertise in special needs and education. The longer you work as *tzadik or tzadikah,* the more familiar you will become with certain special needs and strategies to assist students. However, it is important to rely on the expertise of the learning consultant to make the larger decisions for students in your school.

2. Whenever you notice something that doesn't feel comfortable in your classroom, as an advocate for students you have the right and responsibility to point it out to the administration. When this occurs, you should first think about who the best person to contact is. Usually, you should speak to your learning consultant. Sometimes, he or she sees the same issue, but has determined that it is not necessary to correct at that time.

3. Even though you have learned successful strategies for your own student, it is important to remember that your teacher is the ultimate authority in your classroom. Though it is always helpful to share successful strategies with your teacher, be careful to respect proper boundaries with your teacher.

4. You have been given many tools for assisting students. Though teachers are typically trained in classroom management, often they cannot see what you observe as a second leader in the classroom. Sharing strategies in a respectful manner with your teacher is helpful to your school.

5. You should always remember that it is the learning consultant's job to discuss special needs with parents. Though you feel it may be helpful to share information with other parents, there are many legal issues that go along with sharing too much information. Speaking with another parent is not your role as a *tzadik or tzadikah.*

Congratulations! You are now another key advocate for your student and for other children at your synagogue who may also have special needs. Remember how important this role is. Your student is able to have a meaningful and positive Jewish experience because of what you are doing to help him or her succeed in the classroom. Hopefully, you are starting to develop a strong I-Thou relationship with your student as well.

WORKSHOP III

Self-Study Exercises

(to be completed prior to attending Workshop III)

Have you ever counted the days waiting for something exciting, only to become disappointed when that time arrives? Sometimes, our expectations do not live up to reality. So, too, reality sets in the more you work with your student.

As the months have passed and you and your student have become familiar with each other's ways, hopefully a positive routine has developed. Though a plan has been set out for you, even the best strategies do not always produce the most effective results.

Describe a situation in which you knew you helped your student.

Describe your feelings when you succeeded.

Describe a situation when you feel your assistance did not work.

Describe your feelings when you feel you failed.

WORKSHOP III

Reevaluating Your Student's Needs

Objectives: By the end of this workshop, you will be able to:

- Evaluate the success of current teaching strategies.
- Understand the steps to take when certain strategies in a learning plan are no longer successful.
- Understand that the learning needs of students change often as they mature.
- Apply new learning strategies in consultation with the learning consultant/educational director as needed (the "TASC" plan).

Evaluating the Success of Current Teaching Strategies

At the beginning of this program, you must have been overwhelmed by your new responsibility. You were given information about a student with special needs and a learning plan (or you had to develop your own), and then you were thrust into a classroom to assist your student in adjusting to a new classroom situation. Now that half of the school year is almost over, it is time to take a step back and see how things are progressing. Is your student's learning plan still meeting his or her needs? Are all the classroom modifications still necessary? Have you experimented with different techniques, or sought assistance from others? This workshop is designed to help you through the process of evaluating your student's learning plan.

Learning Plan Evaluation Exercise

In order to complete this exercise, you are going to need a copy of your student's learning plan and some foil star stickers. Quickly reread through the learning plan. Then go back and place a star sticker next to each strategy that you are still using consistently with your student.

Which strategy, in particular, do you find most helpful and why? _____

____

____

____

____

____

Now, pair up with another *tzadik(ah)*. Share with him or her a specific classroom situation in which you used this strategy noted on your classroom learning plan and how the strategy was successful. Explain how you feel your student benefited from this intervention.

Wisdom from Our Sages

Moses sat as a magistrate among the people, while the people stood around Moses from morning until evening. But when Moses's father-in-law [Jethro] saw how much Moses had to do for the people, he said, "What is this thing that you are doing to the people? Why do you act alone, while all the people stand around you from morning until evening?"

Exodus 18:13–15

Moses's father-in-law said to him, "The thing you are doing is not right; you will surely wear yourself out, and these people as well. For the task is too heavy for you—you cannot do it alone."

Exodus 18:17–18

You shall also seek out from among all the people capable men who fear God, trustworthy men who spurn ill-gotten gain. Set these over them as chiefs of thousands, hundreds, fifties, and tens, and let them judge the people at all times. Have them bring every major dispute to you, but let them decide every minor dispute themselves. Make it easier for yourself by letting them share the burden with you.

Exodus 18:21–22

Just before Moses ascended Mount Sinai to receive the Ten Commandments, he learned a powerful lesson from his father-in-law.

What was the lesson that Moses learned? ____________________

____

____

____

____

____

____

Though we often feel an obligation to complete a task ourselves, sometimes situations require collaboration. Though Moses was the leader of the Israelites, he quickly learned that a true leader seeks advice and assistance from others.

The leader of your program has followed Jethro's advice in creating the tzadikim program at your school. How is this program similar to the text above? ______________________________

____

____

____

____

____

How might you follow Jethro's advice working as a tzadik(ah)?

____

____

____

____

____

When Something Is Just Not Working

Now that you have spent time examining what works, take a look at the strategies that did not get stars. List them below:

____

____

____

____

____

____

____

____

Should you keep trying these strategies just because they are stated on your learning plan? The answer is yes and no. There is a process to follow before disregarding a strategy. Though you have powerful insight in your direct contact with your student, you must also consult with others who will help you make these important decisions. The process for reevaluating a student's learning plan is a simple one—you just have to remember the "TASC" at hand:

T ry the strategy again, even if it fails the first few times.
A sk your supervisor or teacher for help.
S hare the techniques that have been successful.
C ollaborate to find a new strategy.

Try again, **A**sk, **S**hare, **C**ollaborate. Through this task (TASC), you will find the most successful plan for your student.

Learning Needs of Students Often Change As They Mature

As your student is growing and maturing, his or her needs are changing as well. Some of the most successful strategies can break down overnight as students begin to see the world through more mature eyes.

Applying What You Learned

> Justin (your student) is a third grader. Last year he worked with a *tzadik* using a behavior chart. The *tzadik* gave him stars throughout the day to help reinforce good behaviors. At the beginning of this year, you were instructed on the learning plan to use a behavior chart with Justin again. Justin liked his behavior chart at the beginning of the year, but now he keeps telling you that he does not need it. The more time you have spent with him, the more you realize that his behaviors are improving and you are able to help him participate in classroom activities using the other strategies you were taught during orientation. What should you do? Should you continue using the behavior chart with Justin?

Write down what you would do to cover each step of this "TASC":

T ____

A ____

S ____

C ____

Discuss this case as a group. Are there certain ages when behavior charts no longer work? Is it the same for every child? Could you readapt the concept of a behavior chart into another system? How?

Are there any strategies on your current learning plan that are no longer working for your student? If so, what are they?

1. ______________________________

2. ______________________________

3. ______________________________

Why do you think these are no longer working?

____

____

____

____

____

Have you found other strategies that have worked with your student? If yes, list them below. When you finish, share them with the group.

1. ______________________________

2. ______________________________

3. ______________________________

Have you done anything to ensure that your supervisor or teacher knows about the strategies you listed above? If you haven't done anything yet, what should you now do, according to your "TASC" plan? __________

____

____

____

____

____

____

Chevruta Study

Jewish tradition teaches that we learn best when we discuss an issue or a text with a partner. This is called "*chevruta* study." Work with a partner. Each pair should choose at least one scenario. With your partner, read over the student's information and the strategies, and then discuss if the strategy is working, other possible strategies, and where you would go to get assistance, if needed.

Every time Ms. Gold introduces a new activity, Ronny, your first-grade student, seems like he is lost in space. Ronny's learning plan suggests that you repeat directions to him. When the teacher gives directions, you try to do this, but he still seems to still be lost. This time, you decide to . . .

The learning plan for your second-grader, Leslie, suggests that you take Leslie for short walks as frequent breaks to help her re-focus. She loves going on walks with you; however, you find that her time out of the classroom seems to actually cause her to have more problems reorienting and focusing on the activity at hand once you get back in the classroom. Upon reentering the classroom this time, you . . .

Michael, your third-grade student, tells you that he is embarrassed that you always sit right next to him. He asks if you can sit in the back of the classroom instead. You're not sure if you will be able to carry out your assigned strategies if you are so far away, but you also want to respect his feelings. So you . . .

Allison seems to be falling significantly behind in Hebrew class. You are following all the suggestions on her learning plan, but she is not learning any of the Hebrew letters and you are growing concerned. Her second-grade year is now more than half over. As you are working today, you decide to . . .

Dylan is the only pre-K student in the class who can't sit still. His learning plan states that when Dylan is fidgety, he should be allowed to move around. Mrs. Wasser has asked you to try to keep him in his seat. Nothing you try seems to work. At this point, you . . .

After *chevruta* study, answer the following questions as a group.

- Was the original strategy fully implemented?
- Was it successful?
- If not, why did the strategy fail?
- Should the *tzadik(ah)* try it again?
- How might he or she try it in a different way?
- What other strategies may work better in this situation?

WORKSHOP IV

Self-Study Exercises

(to be completed prior to attending Workshop IV)

The goal of the *tzadikim* program is not only to help students with learning differences succeed in religious school, but also to help create the next generation of Jewish educational leaders. The skills you have developed during the school year are skills that cannot be acquired in even the highest-level college courses. Your hands-on experience over this past year will help you succeed in high school and beyond.

The Mishnah teaches that* mitzvah goreret mitzvah *or "one mitzvah leads to another"* (Pirkei Avot 4:2)*. What do you think this rabbinic verse means and how might it be related to your work during the school year? ______

____

____

____

When a student practices a skill regularly, not only does he or she become better at it, but it slowly becomes a natural and comfortable part of his or her approach to learning. The more you practice the skills you have learned as a *tzadik(ah)*, the more they will become part of your regular teaching style. Hopefully, your experience this year will lead you to a lifetime of positive teaching and modeling skills, as well as a desire to help and advocate for others.

In addition, in the time that you and your student have spent together you should have forged a mutually beneficial relationship. Just as your student has grown from your help, you have also grown in many ways.

How have you seen your student grow (physically, intellectually, or emotionally) since the beginning of the year? ______________________

____

____

____

How do you feel that you have grown (physically, intellectually, or emotionally)? ______________________________

____

____

____

____

____

____

To prepare for the upcoming session, briefly describe two or three memorable (both positive and negative) episodes or experiences with your student. Do not worry about writing in complete sentences.

____

____

____

____

____

____

____

____

____

____

WORKSHOP IV

Planning for the Next School Year and Self-evaluation

Objectives: By the end of this workshop, you will:

- Evaluate your student's growth over the current year.
- Provide input for a learning plan for the next school year.
- Recognize your growth as a special needs facilitator.
- Understand how your role as a *tzadik(ah)* relates to your Jewish spiritual growth.

As the end of the school year is approaching, this workshop will give you the opportunity to assist in planning for your student for the upcoming school year, as well as to evaluate your own growth during this past school year. In Workshop III, you were given the task of reevaluating your student's needs. Now take that a step further. The following questionnaire is designed to assist you in evaluating your student holistically from the start to the end of this school year.

Evaluating Your Student's Growth

The purpose of this questionnaire is to evaluate your student's growth in the following three areas since the beginning of this school year:

- Behavior
- Learning
- Social/Emotional Development

Use the following five-point scale to answer the questions:

5 – Excellent
4 – Above Average
3 – Average
2 – Below Average
1 – Poor

Circle a 1, 2, 3, 4, or 5 following each question.

SECTION 1: BEHAVIOR

1. At the very beginning of the school year, how would you rate your student's general classroom behavior when under your direct supervision?

   1 2 3 4 5

2. By the middle of the school year, how would you rate your student's general classroom behavior when under your direct supervision?

   1 2 3 4 5

3. How would you now rate your student's general classroom behavior when under your direct supervision?

   1 2 3 4 5

4. At the very beginning of the school year, how would you rate your student's ability to focus and pay attention when under your direct supervision?

   1 2 3 4 5

5. By the middle of the school year, how would you rate your student's ability to focus and pay attention when under your direct supervision?

   1 2 3 4 5

6. How would you now rate your student's general classroom ability to focus and pay attention when under your direct supervision?

   1 2 3 4 5

Did your student's general classroom behavior improve since the beginning of the year? Why or why not? ____________________

____

____

____

Did your student's ability to focus and pay attention improve since the beginning of the year? Why or why not? ______________________________

____

____

____

____

SECTION 2: LEARNING

1. At the very beginning of the school year, how would you rate your student's general ability to grasp new concepts when under your direct supervision?

   1 2 3 4 5

2. By the middle of the school year, how would you rate your student's general ability to grasp new concepts when under your direct supervision?

   1 2 3 4 5

3. How would you now rate your student's general ability to grasp new concepts when under your direct supervision?

   1 2 3 4 5

4. At the very beginning of the school year, how would you rate your student's overall retention level of the material presented by his or her teacher(s)?

   1 2 3 4 5

5. By the middle of the school year, how would you rate your student's overall retention level of the material presented by his or her teacher(s)?

   1 2 3 4 5

6. How would you now rate your student's overall retention level of the material presented by his or her teacher(s)?

   1 2 3 4 5

Did your student's general ability to grasp new concepts improve since the beginning of the year? Why or why not? ______________________

____

____

____

____

Did your student's overall retention of the material presented by his or her teacher(s) improve since the beginning of the year? Why or why not? ____

____

____

____

____

SECTION 3: SOCIAL/EMOTIONAL DEVELOPMENT

1. At the very beginning of the school year, how would you rate your student's overall maturity?

   1 2 3 4 5

2. By the middle of the school year, how would you rate your student's overall maturity?

   1 2 3 4 5

3. How would you now rate your student's overall maturity?

   1 2 3 4 5

4. At the very beginning of the school year, how would you rate your student's ability to make friends and socialize with the other students?

   1 2 3 4 5

5. By the middle of the school year, how would you rate your student's ability to make friends and socialize with the other students?

   1 2 3 4 5

6. How would you now rate your student's ability to make friends and socialize with the other students?

   1 2 3 4 5

Did your student's overall maturity improve since the beginning of the year? Why or why not? ______________________________

____

____

____

____

Did your student's ability to make friends and socialize with the other students improve since the beginning of the year? Why or why not?

____

____

____

____

____

You have probably learned many things from the questionnaire. Likely, your confidence and ability to anticipate your student's needs, and monitor and provide appropriate interventions, have helped your student to show improvement in at least one of the three areas on which you just reflected. It is also likely that your student has grown and matured through the year and is perhaps requiring fewer interventions and demonstrating more frequent success in the classroom. Yet there is also a possibility that due to circumstances beyond your control and/or a complex developmental or learning disability, your student has made no notable improvements in any of these three areas. If this is the case, it is important to reflect on what your interventions have accomplished. Would your student be able to participate in a regular classroom without you present? Has your student benefited from being in a Jewish environment and having positive Jewish experiences as a direct result of your presence? The answer to both of these questions is yes.

Work with a partner and share the results of your student evaluation.

Finalizing the Learning Plan

In Workshop III, you reevaluated your student's learning plan by placing foil stars next to the items you would continue to utilize as well as noting which interventions were no longer necessary. You also noted additional interventions that you found effective. As you approach the end of the year, and with the completion of the evaluation questionnaire, revisit your student's learning plan one more time.

Review your notes from Workshop III, assess your student's most recent progress, and utilize this knowledge to "finalize" what you think your student's learning plan should look like for the next school year (the actual learning plan will be determined by the learning consultant, with input from parents, teachers, and especially the *tzadik* or *tzadikah*). Use a pen or pencil to cross out any interventions you find do not work anymore and rank those that are effective in order of importance (i.e., place a number 1 next to the most effective strategy, a number 2 next the second most effective strategy, and so on). If you use strategies not currently listed on the learning plan, write them down on the bottom or the back of the page. Take ten minutes to complete this exercise individually then turn in your finalized version to your supervisor for review.

Recognizing Your Growth as a Special Needs Facilitator

As you have probably discovered this year, everyone learns differently. Some people are oral learners and others are visual learners. Some people learn by doing and others like to learn from a book. But as a special needs facilitator, you have learned a great deal by seeing the world through another person's eyes. And as you have gained an awareness of the way students learn, you have probably discovered that we all have learning differences. This means that you have become a much more empathetic young adult.

But empathy is not the only skill you have gained through this program. Using the same five-point system you used to evaluate your student's growth throughout the school year, assess how you have grown this year. You will be evaluating your growth over the year in the following four areas:

- Patience
- Leadership
- Empathy
- Being a Role Model

As a reminder, use the following five-point scale to answer the questions:

5 – Excellent
4 – Above Average
3 – Average
2 – Below Average
1 – Poor

Circle a 1, 2, 3, 4, or 5 following each question.

SECTION 1: PATIENCE

1. At the very beginning of the school year, how would you rate your overall patience when working with your student?

   1 2 3 4 5

2. By the middle of the school year, how would you rate your overall patience when working with your student?

   1 2 3 4 5

3. How would you now rate your overall patience when working with your student?

   1 2 3 4 5

SECTION 2: LEADERSHIP

1. At the very beginning of the school year, how would you rate your overall leadership skills?

   1 2 3 4 5

2. By the middle of the school year, how would you rate your overall leadership skills?

   1 2 3 4 5

3. How would you now rate your overall leadership skills?

   1 2 3 4 5

SECTION 3: EMPATHY

1. At the very beginning of the school year, how would you rate your overall empathy for those with learning differences?

   1 2 3 4 5

2. By the middle of the school year, how would you rate your overall empathy for those with learning differences?

   1 2 3 4 5

3. How would you now rate your overall empathy for those with learning differences?

   1 2 3 4 5

SECTION 4: BEING A ROLE MODEL

1. How would you rate yourself as a role model at the very beginning of the school year?

   1 2 3 4 5

2. How would you rate yourself as a role model in the middle of the school year?

   1 2 3 4 5

3. How would you now rate yourself as a role model?

   1 2 3 4 5

Read the following adjectives. Place a check next to each of the adjectives that describe you as a leader.

___ empathetic	___ caring	___ intuitive	___ strong
___ fair	___ religious	___ intelligent	___ observant
___ focused	___ organized	___ authoritative	___ charismatic
___ compassionate	___ admirable	___ modest	___ polished
___ thoughtful	___ talented	___ generous	___ passionate
___ dynamic	___ honest	___ resourceful	___ loyal
___ patriotic	___ gregarious	___ mindful	___ cautious
___ sincere	___ gracious	___ praiseworthy	___ trustworthy
___ ethical	___ commendable	___ humble	___ daring

When you apply to college and go on job interviews, you are often asked to describe your leadership skills. For most people, this is not an easy task. However, by evaluating your growth as a *tzadik(ah)*, you have identified some of your leadership skills.

Using the four evaluation sections above, in addition to the list of adjectives, write a paragraph describing your leadership skills as a special needs facilitator. Present yourself as if you were applying for a job.

____

____

____

____

____

____

____

Understanding How Your Role as a Tzadik(ah) Relates to Your Jewish Spiritual Growth

> "Man was given a share in His wisdom and is called to responsible living and to be a partner of God in the redemption of the world."
>
> —Abraham Joshua Heschel (*God in Search of Man*, p. 66)

Abraham Joshua Heschel, one of the greatest Jewish thinkers of the twentieth century, often spoke about our role as God's partners in bettering the world. God gives a special talent to every living creature. Some of us excel in sports, some in academics, some in art. Others have the gift of humor or are good at problem solving. Your gift of compassion and dedication to helping others makes you God's partner in perfecting the world. Whether you are a regular synagogue attendee or not, you possess a divine spark within you that helps bring our world one step closer to perfection. Working with students with special needs makes you a very holy and spiritual person, whether you knew it or not!
Complete these sentences.

When I work with my student, I feel ______________________________

When I perform this mitzvah, I feel a connection with God because

After studying to be a tzadik(ah) ***this year, I have learned that Judaism teaches*** ______________________________

Conclusion

Through your work this year, you have learned new skills and touched the life of a student with special needs in ways that you may never even know. Your two to three hours together each week have demonstrated that Jewish learning is possible for every type of learner. You have stretched beyond your comfort zone and have grown tremendously as a leader and a mensch.

As you move on to other challenges in life, use the knowledge from your experiences this year to guide you through them. As you see others struggle in this world, do your best to encourage them as you have encouraged your student. And as you look at yourself in the mirror from now on, see if you can see the same leadership skills that your student sees in you each week.

Though your task as a religious school *tzadik(ah)* is complete, your gifts to the world have just begun. May you be blessed in all your endeavors in life and may you continue to bless those whom you help in this world.

Acknowledgments

There are so many people who have shown us the importance of welcoming everyone throughout our lives. Starting with our parents and grandparents, we were taught in our early years to give of ourselves and our resources to make a difference in others' lives. This is a message that we continue to pass on to both Steven's children Aviv, Ohad, Amit, Reid, and Matthew and Stacey's children Ari and Jolie.

Zissy Pozin first introduced Steven to the idea that every child learns differently and deserves to be taught "al pi darco," according to his or her own way and Zena Sulkes gave him the tools to get down on the level of each and every learner. Stacey's love for both Judaism and working with children who learn differently is credited to her two loving parents, Morris and Judy Gurevitch. Her parents constantly nurtured her passions, and guided her toward finding her professional career which brings fulfillment to her life. Stacey is forever grateful for their constant guidance, love and support.

We are blessed to have so many people in our lives who have supported us in our work and our writing. We especially thank The Temple Hebrew Benevolent Congregation, its dynamic clergy and leadership, Rabbi Alvin Sugarman, members of the 2003-4 Religious School Committee, Sheila Regal, the Jewish Federation of Greater Atlanta, Elizabeth Foster, Stephanie Fields, Denny Marcus, Dr. Jane Wilkov, Elizabeth McGarry, Jason Crutcher, Georgia Kimmel, Abby Bocinec, Loretta Shapiro, and all of the *tzadikim* over the past twelve years who helped lay the groundwork for this important work in the future of inclusive Jewish education. We are so grateful for Michael Goldberg and URJ Press, who fully understand the need and importance of Jewish inclusive education.

And most of all, we are blessed to come home each night to the two most supportive spouses, who both teach us and our children empathy and love, Julie and Eric.

We are blessed by all of you.

About the Authors

STEVEN H. RAU, RJE, is the director of lifelong learning at The Temple in Atlanta, Georgia. He is a rabbi and graduate of Hebrew Union College–Jewish Institute of Religion and holds a master's degree in educational leadership. A passionate believer in inclusive education, he teaches, preaches, and models the message that synagogues should strive to be the first gateway of inclusion for all learners. Steven lives with his wife Julie in Atlanta with their five children, Aviv, Ohad, Amit, Reid, and Matthew.

STACEY LEVY, M.S., CCC-SLP, is a speech-language pathologist with over 17 years of experience in her field. In addition to her full-time work running her successful practice, she is a State of Georgia "Bright from the Start" certified presenter and oversees The Temple's Yad B'Yad Inclusive Education Program. Stacey received her bachelor of science in education from the University of Wisconsin, Madison, in 1995. She earned her master of science in communication disorders from the University of Texas at Dallas, Callier Center for Communication Disorders, in 1997. She and her husband Eric live in Atlanta with their children, Ari and Jolie.

To download a PDF of "Learning to Be a *Tzadik*" (the tzadikim training manual), visit URJBooksandMusic.com/EveryoneIsWelcome and enter password "welcome" when prompted.